English in Action
Workbook

Barbara H. Foley

Elizabeth R. Neblett

THOMSON ™

HEINLE

Australia • Canada • Mexico • Singapore • Spain • United Kingdom • United States

THOMSON
HEINLE

English in Action 4, Workbook
by Barbara H. Foley, Elizabeth R. Neblett

Publisher, Adult and Academic ESL: *James W. Brown*
Senior Acquisitions Editor: *Sherrise Roehr*
Developmental Editor: *Sarah Barnicle*
Assistant Editor: *Audra Longert*
Editorial Assistant: *Katherine Reilly*
Senior Marketing Manager,
  Adult ESL: *Donna Lee Kennedy*
Director, Global ESL Training &
  Development: *Evelyn Nelson*
Senior Production Editor: *Maryellen Killeen*
Senior Frontlist Buyer: *Mary Beth Hennebury*
Project Manager: *Tünde A. Dewey*

Compositor: *Pre-Press Co., Inc.*
Text Printer/Binder: *West Group*
Text Designer: *Sue Gerald*
Cover Designer: *Gina Petti/Rotunda Design House*
Photo Researcher: *Jill Engerbretson*
Photography Manager: *Sheri Blaney*
Cover Art: *Zita Asbaghi/* **Unit Opener Art:** *Zita Asbaghi*
Illustrators: *Scott MacNeill; Ray Medici;*
  Glen Giron, Roger Acaya, Ibarra
  Cristostomo, Leo Cultura of Raketshop
  Design Studio, Philippines

 Photo Credits

All photos courtesy of Elizabeth R. Neblett with the following exceptions:

Page 2, top: ©Table Mesa Prod./Index Stock Imagery
Page 17: ©Yang Liu/CORBIS
Page 29: ©Yvette Cardoza/Index Stock Imagery
Page 43: ©Chris Hamilton/CORBIS
Page 69: ©Todd Bigelow/AURORA
Page 81: ©Ryan McVay/PhotoDisc/Getty Images
Page 82: ©PhotoDisc/Getty Images
Page 86, left: ©AFP/CORBIS
Page 86, middle: ©Reuters NewMedia Inc./CORBIS
Page 86, right: ©AFP/CORBIS
Page 87: ©Jim Lake/CORBIS
Page 89: ©Reuters NewMedia Inc./CORBIS
Page 90: ©AP/Photo/Reed Saxon
Page 91: ©Courtesy of Music Central Management

Contents

Education

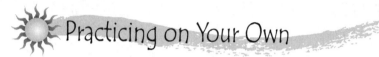

Practicing on Your Own

1. Complete the sentences that describe each picture. Use the present continuous tense and the verbs in parentheses. Some of the sentences are negative. Then, write one new sentence.

1. The students _____ are writing _____ (write).

2. They _____ (take) a test.

3. They _____ (sit) in their classroom.

4. _____

5. The students _____ (work) in the college library.

6. The students _____ (research) information on computers.

7. None of the students _____ (print) information right now.

8. _____

9. All of the students _____ (stand) in front of the board.

10. One woman _____ (read) words to her classmates.

11. They _____ (write) sentences.

12. _____

2. Complete the sentences about schools in your native country. Use the simple present tense of the verbs in parentheses. Use negative verbs when necessary.

1. Students _____ (attend) school during the summer.

2. Elementary school students _____ (take) the bus to school.

3. A typical school _____ (have) air conditioning.

4. High schools _____ (offer) after-school sports.

5. A typical female student _____ (participate) in after-school sports.

6. A teacher _____ (wear) jeans to class.

7. A parent _____ (meet) the teachers more than once a year.

8. Elementary school teachers _____ (call) parents when there is a problem.

3. Write five sentences about the school where you study English.

1. _____

2. _____

3. _____

4. _____

5. _____

4. Complete the sentences about your class using adverbs of frequency and the verbs in parentheses.

Adverbs of frequency					
Place adverbs of frequency after the verb *be* and before all other verbs.					
He is *never* on time.			He *always* arrives late.		
always 100% usually 90%	frequently/often 70–80% sometimes 50%		rarely/seldom 10–20% almost never 5%		never 0%

1. I _____ (be) late for class.

2. I _____ (study) before I take a test.

3. My classmates and I _____ (speak) English in class.

4. My homework _____ (be) neat.

5. I _____ (use) a computer to type my homework.

6. If I don't understand something, I _____ (ask) the teacher.

7. My classmates and I _____ (work) in groups.

5. **Read this story about the three students in the picture. Fill in the correct form of the verbs in parentheses. Use the present continuous or the simple present form.**

Student Center

premed—A premed student plans to attend medical school. Premed students take science courses such as biology, chemistry, and psychology.

Charlie, Ahmed, and Michelle _____**are studying**_____ (study) in the student center today. They _____ (study/usually) in the library, but this afternoon they _____ (need) to talk and there _____ (be/not) a place for them in the library. Today, they _____ (prepare) for a biology exam. Their biology instructor _____ (give/always) difficult exams, so they _____ (try) to test each other. Charlie _____ _____ (ask) questions, and Ahmed and Michelle _____ _____ (take) turns answering the questions.

Michelle _____ (want) to get an A in the biology course and so do Ahmed and Charlie. They _____ (be) premed students and _____ (want) to apply to medical school in the future. Premed students _____ (need) good grades in biology and other sciences, so Michelle, Ahmed, and Charlie _____ _____ (spend) the day in the student center preparing for the exam. Other students in the student center _____ (watch) TV or _____ (play) video games, but Charlie, Ahmed, and Michelle _____ (pay/not) any attention to them. They are focused on their studies.

6. Write questions about the story on page 4. Use the cues.

1. Where **are they studying?**
   (they/study)
   Answer: In the student center.

2. Where _____
   (they/study/usually)
   Answer: In the library.

3. _____
   (be/place to talk in the library)
   Answer: No, there isn't.

4. What kind of exam _____
   (they/prepare for)
   Answer: A biology exam.

5. _____
   (biology professor/give/difficult exams)
   Answer: Yes, she does.

6. What _____
   (they/do)
   Answer: They're testing each other.

7. Who _____
   (ask/questions)
   Answer: Charlie is.

8. Who _____
   (answer/questions)
   Answer: Ahmed and Michelle are.

9. Who _____
   (need/good grades)
   Answer: They all do.

10. Where _____
    (they/spend the day)
    Answer: In the student center.

11. Who _____
    (watch TV)
    Answer: Other students are.

7. Listen and circle Now or Every day.

1. Now	Every day		**5.** Now		Every day
2. Now	Every day		**6.** Now		Every day
3. Now	Every day		**7.** Now		Every day
4. Now	Every day		**8.** Now		Every day

8. Listen and write a short answer.

Yes, it is.	Yes, there is.	Yes, it does.	Yes, they are.
No, it isn't.	No, there isn't.	No, it doesn't.	No, they aren't.

1. _____   **5.** _____

2. _____   **6.** _____

3. _____   **7.** _____

4. _____   **8.** _____

9. Listen to the description of Miami-Dade Community College. Take notes.

Notes

Number of campuses: _____   Year founded: _____

Annual enrollment: _____   International students: _____

Faculty: _____   Full-time tuition: _____

Degrees and programs: _____

_____

Activities for students: _____

_____

Circle T for True or F for False.

1. Miami-Dade is a private college.	T	F
2. The college has six campuses.	T	F
3. It has 55,000 international students.	T	F
4. All students pay the same tuition.	T	F

5. Anyone who wants to can attend Miami-Dade.   T   F

6. The college offers bachelor's degrees.   T   F

7. The college offers certificate programs.   T   F

8. All of the students speak Spanish.   T   F

9. Students can live in dormitories on campus.   T   F

Reading: Applying to a Four-Year College in the United States

In the United States, there are many types of schools of higher education. There are four-year colleges and universities that offer bachelor's degrees and graduate degrees. There are two-year community colleges and junior colleges that offer associate's degrees and certificates. There are also technical schools that teach students specific skills for jobs as electricians, plumbers, beauticians, and auto mechanics. There is a school for every type of student.

Some schools have "open admission," which means they accept anyone who applies. Others select their students, using applications, references, and other factors. Admissions officers of the colleges look at the applications carefully. Here is some of the information that students have to include on their applications:

- What is your previous education (secondary/high school, certificates, other diplomas, etc.)?
- What extracurricular activities do you participate in (e.g., clubs or teams)?
- What volunteer work or community service do you participate in?
- Describe your work history.
- Describe your most interesting work or educational experience.
- Why do you want to attend this school?

Imagine that you are applying to a four-year college. In the space below, answer two of the questions above.

1. _____

_____

_____

_____

_____

2. _____

_____

_____

_____

_____

Colonial Times
(1607–1776)

Practicing on Your Own

1. Compare life today with life in colonial times. Read the sentence about life today. Use the cues to write about life in colonial times.

1. Today, the population is about half male and half female. (six men for each woman)

   In colonial times, there were six men for each woman.

2. Most people travel by car. (walk from place to place)

   Most people walked from place to place.

3. Most families have one or two children. (six or seven children)

4. Most people have watches. (few people)

5. People gather around the TV at night. (fireplace)

6. Most homes have six or seven rooms. (one or two)

7. There are one or more bathrooms in homes. (no bathrooms)

8. There is no smallpox in the United States. (smallpox/common)

9. Roads are paved. (rough and muddy)

10. People often travel. (rarely)

11. Few people wear wigs. (men, women, and children/wigs)

12. People wash their clothes frequently. (once a month)

2. The presidents. Complete the sentences below with *was* or *were*.

1st George Washington	1789–1797	No political party
3rd Thomas Jefferson	1801–1809	Democratic Republican
16th Abraham Lincoln	1861–1865	Republican
32nd Franklin D. Roosevelt	1933–1945	Democrat
35th John F. Kennedy	1961–1963	Democrat
37th Richard Nixon	1969–1974	Republican
40th Ronald Reagan	1981–1989	Republican
41st George H. W. Bush	1989–1993	Republican
42nd William Clinton	1993–2001	Democrat
43rd George W. Bush	2001–	Republican

1. George Washington _____ the first president of the United States.

2. John F. Kennedy _____ the youngest president. Ronald Reagan _____ the oldest. He _____ 78 years old when he left office.

3. Many recent presidents _____ governors before they became presidents.

4. Richard Nixon _____ the only president to resign.

5. Kennedy and Nixon _____ the first two candidates to debate on TV.

6. Many presidents _____ lawyers before they became presidents.

7. Franklin D. Roosevelt _____ president during World War II.

3. Answer these questions about the information in the chart on the presidents.

1. ___Was___ George Washington a Democrat? ___No, he wasn't.___

2. _____ Washington the first president of the United States? _____

3. _____ Jefferson president from 1797 to 1809? _____

4. _____ Abraham Lincoln a Republican? _____

5. _____ Lincoln president for eight years? _____

6. _____ Lincoln and Roosevelt from the same party? _____

7. _____ Kennedy in office one full term? _____

8. _____ Nixon and Reagan Democrats? _____

9. _____ William Clinton president for two terms? _____

1650	The main form of transportation was horse and wagon. It took six to ten weeks to sail across the Atlantic Ocean from England to New York.
1830	Passengers rode on the first railroad train in the United States in Charleston, South Carolina. In 1830, there were 23 miles of railroad track. By 1840, there were 3,000 miles of railroad track.
1869	The first transcontinental railroad connected the east coast and the west coast. Passengers could travel from New York to San Francisco.
1897	The first subway line in the United States opened in Boston, Massachusetts.
1903	The Wright Brothers made the first airplane flight in Kitty Hawk, North Carolina. The flight was only 12 seconds long. By 1908, the Wright brothers could fly for over one hour.
1908	Henry Ford introduced the Model T, the first affordable automobile. Thousands of people bought the Model T for $850.
1914	The first commercial airline service flew passengers from Tampa to St. Petersburg, Florida.
1929	Charles Lindberg became the first person to fly solo across the Atlantic Ocean. Ten years later, there were regular transcontinental flights.
1961	Russian Cosmonaut Yuri Gagarin was the first person in space. He completed one orbit around the earth in *Vostok I*.
1969	Neil Armstrong became the first person to walk on the moon.

4. Write the short answers.

Was the first airplane flight very short?	Yes, it was.
Were there 3,000 miles of track in 1840?	Yes, there were.
Did the Wright brothers develop the airplane?	Yes, they did.
Could people travel easily in 1800?	No, they couldn't.

1. Did people travel by horse in the 1700s? _____

2. Could people travel by train in 1820? _____

3. Were there 30,000 miles of track by 1840? _____

4. Could people take a train across the U.S. in 1850? _____

5. Was the first airplane flight in 1903? _____

6. Was the first airplane flight an hour long? _____

7. Could the Wright brothers fly for one hour by 1908? _____

8. Did Henry Ford introduce the Model T? _____

9. Did thousands of people buy the Model T? _____

10. Was the first subway in New York City? _____

5. Use the information in the chart to answer the questions about transportation from colonial times to today.

1. How did people use to travel before 1800?

   _____

2. Where was the first railroad line in the United States?

   _____

3. When did the first railroad connect the east and the west?

   _____

4. Where was the first subway line?

   _____

5. How long was the first airplane flight?

   _____

6. How much did a Model T cost in 1908?

   _____

7. Where did the first commercial airline offer service?

   _____

8. Who was the first person to fly solo across the Atlantic Ocean?

   _____

9. When was transcontinental airline service available?

   _____

10. Who was the first person in space?

    _____

11. What did Neil Armstrong do?

    _____

12. How did people travel to America in 1650?

    _____

13. How long did it take to cross the Atlantic Ocean in 1650?

    _____

14. How do most people travel to the United States today?

    _____

15. How many hours does it take to fly from your country
    to the United States?

    _____

6. Compare life today with life fifty years ago. Write each sentence you hear next to the correct answer.

1. _____ Today, many people wear contacts.

2. _Police used to match fingerprints._ Today, they match DNA.

3. _____ Today, they watch color TV.

4. _____ Today, they use computers.

5. _____ Today, it costs $8.00 or more.

7. The box below includes the names of several presidents. Read the statements under the box. Then, listen and write the name of the correct president.

Franklin D. Roosevelt	Bill Clinton	Richard Nixon
John Adams	John Quincy Adams	Ronald Reagan
George W. Bush	George H. W. Bush	George Washington

1. He was the only president to leave office. _____

2. He was in office longer than any other president. _____

3. He was a movie actor. _____

4. He was the first president to live in the White House. _____

5. His wife was elected to political office. _____

6. These presidents also had fathers who were presidents.

_____ _____

8. Listen and write each question you hear next to the correct answer.

1. _____ With my cousin.

2. _____ Yes, I came by myself.

3. _____ In 2001.

4. _____ No, I couldn't.

5. _____ I was 24.

6. _What country are you from?_ I'm from China.

7. _____ No, it wasn't.

Read these sentences about life in colonial America.

1. They settled along the east coast from the area of Maine to Georgia.

2. It wasn't a good area for farming.

3. Therefore, plantation owners began to buy slaves from Africa.

4. As a result, many Native Americans moved farther west.

5. However, when they arrived in America, they did not grant religious freedom to other colonists.

6. In the other colonies, parents taught their children at home.

7. This city, St. Augustine, is the oldest city in the United States.

Now, read this story about life in colonial America. Some of the information is missing. Put the number of the correct sentence from the list above on the correct line in each paragraph.

For thousands of years, Native Americans lived in America. They hunted, farmed, and often moved from place to place. When the colonists arrived, they usually took the land from the Native Americans or paid them very little for it. ____4____.

The English were not the first settlers to arrive in America. Spanish soldiers landed in Florida in 1565 and started the first city. _____. The French explored the area that is now Canada. Both Quebec and Montreal began as French forts in the early 1600s.

The English were the first people to begin large settlements in America. _____. Life was different in the three areas that we now call the New England colonies (the colonies in the north), the Middle colonies, and the Southern colonies.

In the New England colonies, people formed small towns. In the other colonies, homes were far apart. In the New England colonies, towns with fifty or more families started small schools. _____. Parents with money hired private tutors. Children learned to read the Bible and to keep the family accounts.

The weather in the New England colonies was cold and the winters were long. _____. The Middle and Southern colonies had good weather for farming. In the Southern colonies, settlers developed very large farms, called plantations. They needed more workers for the land. _____. The slaves had no rights or freedom. The New England colonies and Middle colonies had very few slaves. In Massachusetts, many of the new settlers were Puritans. They left England for religious freedom. _____. Some colonies granted religious freedom to all. There were differences in the lives of people in the 13 colonies, but as the years went on, people began to see themselves as free and independent.

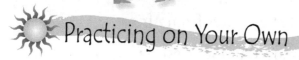

Family Matters

Practicing on Your Own

1. Write two sentences about each picture. Use the future tense with be + *going to* or *will*.

1. He's going to ask her to marry him.

   They will get married next summer.

2. _____

   _____

3. _____

   _____

4. _____

   _____

5. _____

   _____

6. _____

   _____

7. _____

   _____

2. Complete these sentences about your future plans in the affirmative or negative.

1. I _____ attend a friend's wedding soon.
2. I _____ travel around the world.
3. I _____ buy a sports car.
4. I _____ retire in a few years.
5. I _____ look for a new job.
6. I _____ learn how to play the piano.
7. I _____ visit Washington, D.C.
8. I _____ take a vacation next summer.
9. I _____ start my own business someday.
10. I _____ get more exercise.

3. Laura and Gloria are best friends. Laura is flying to her sister's wedding and will be away for one week. Gloria is helping her get ready. Complete their conversation. Use *will* in each offer to help.

Laura: I only have one small suitcase.

Gloria: I'll lend you a suitcase. _____

Laura: I have to be at the airport tomorrow morning at 8:00 A.M.

Gloria: _____

Laura: I forgot to cancel the mail.

Gloria: _____

Laura: I don't have anyone to watch my cat while I'm away.

Gloria: _____

Laura: I have a lot of food in my refrigerator. It's going to go bad.

Gloria: _____

Laura: And I forgot to take this video back to the video rental store.

Gloria: _____

Laura: My new boyfriend is going to be lonely while I'm gone.

Gloria: _____

Laura: My return flight gets in next Saturday at 11:00 P.M.

Gloria: _____

4. Complete these sentences.

1. After Miguel retires, __he's going to move to Florida.__

_____

2. Emily _____

_____ after she graduates.

3. When Gustavo visits his family, _____

_____ .

4. When Joe asks Sylvia to marry him, _____

_____ .

5. Joe and Sylvia _____

_____ after they get married.

6. Before the Acosta family comes to the United States, ____

_____ .

7. Mr. Williams _____

_____ if it rains tommorrow.

5. **Kim lives in New York and Ben lives in Boston. They are planning to get married. Combine these sentences about their plans, using a future time clause and the words in parentheses.**

1. Ben and Kim are going to get married. They are going to live in Boston. (after)

   After Ben and Kim get married, they are going to live in Boston.

2. They are going to get married. Kim is going to quit her job. (before)

   _____

3. Kim is going to look for a job. Kim is going to move to Boston. (when)

   _____

4. Kim is going to move to Boston. Kim is going to take her cat with her. (when)

   _____

5. They are going to get married. Kim is going to keep her own name. (after)

   _____

6. They are going to save for a house. They are going to have children. (before)

   _____

7. Ben is going to look for another job. Ben is going to finish his college degree. (when)

   _____

8. They are going to have time off. They are going to visit different countries. (when)

   _____

9. They are going to have problems. They are going to resolve them together. (when)

   _____

10. Kim is going to stay home. They are going to have children. (if)

    _____

11. The children are going to start school. Kim is going to return to work. (when)

    _____

6. **Before getting married, couples should discuss many important issues. Listen and write the questions.**

1. _____
2. _____
3. _____
4. _____
5. _____
6. _____
7. _____
8. _____
9. _____

7. **Listen to these short conversations. Then, complete the sentences.**

1. When Susan works overtime, _her mother is going to watch the kids_____ .
2. Before they go to the hospital, _____ .
3. He's going to clean his room _____ .
4. She's going to go to the mall _____ .
5. _____ when he's on vacation.
6. After she takes the entrance exam, _____ .
7. _____ before they leave.
8. If he's late again, _____ .

8. **Listen and write the short answers. Use your imagination!**

1. _____   6. _____
2. _____   7. _____
3. _____   8. _____
4. _____   9. _____
5. _____   10. _____

Reading: Arranged Marriages

Are you a single person between the ages of 18 and 30? Would you like your family's help finding a partner to marry? In some countries, families are very involved in helping their young men and women meet and marry the "right" person. This is common in India, Iran, Pakistan, Azerbaijan, and other countries, and is often referred to as an "arranged marriage."

Let's imagine a typical young man in India and name him Pritesh. A man's family believes he is ready to marry when he has finished his education and has begun his career, usually in his mid twenties. Pritesh attended business school and is an accountant in a small firm. His family and friends have their eyes open. They are looking for a young woman who is the same religion, speaks the same language, and is similar in education, wealth, and social level. The family discusses many possible choices: the daughter of a friend, the daughter of Pritesh's father's boss, the daughter of the family's dentist. They may also place an advertisement in the newspaper, describing their son and his many accomplishments. Finally, they hear of a young woman named Ashima in the next town. She is the daughter of a teacher in the local high school. Both sets of parents talk and a meeting is arranged.

Pritesh and his family visit the parents of the young woman. The parents sit and talk. Then, it is time for tea. Ashima walks into the room and serves tea to her family and guests. This is the first time that the young couple sees one another. Meetings are not always at homes. They may also occur at a religious service or at a family event, such as a wedding.

After the meeting, the young people can give their opinions. It's possible to say, "I do not think he/she is right for me." However, Pritesh and Ashima are both interested in continuing the relationship. Within a few weeks, they are engaged. A few months later, they are married. Their marriage has a good chance of succeeding because the young people have so much in common, and they also have the full support of their families.

Circle T for *True* or F for *False* based on the reading.

1. It is common for a man to marry while he is attending college.   T   F

2. In many countries, families want their children to marry a person who practices the same religion.   T   F

3. All parents place an ad in the newspaper.   T   F

4. Young people have to marry the person their parents choose for them.   T   F

5. If two young people are interested in each other, their engagement follows in a few weeks.   T   F

6. The couple can date for several months before they decide to become engaged.   T   F

7. In India, it's important for a couple to fall in love before they marry.   T   F

8. Arranged marriages are common in my native country.   T   F

4 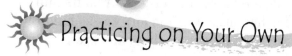 Comparisons— Global and Local

Practicing on Your Own

1. Complete the sentences with the correct comparative or superlative adjective forms.

1. Canada is _____ larger than _____ (large) the United States.

2. Canada is one of _____ the largest countries _____ (large country) in the world.

3. Alaska is _____ (large state) in the United States.

4. New York City is one of _____ (exciting city) in the world.

5. New Mexico is much _____ (hot) Florida.

6. The Yangtze River is _____ (long) the Mississippi River, but the Nile River is _____ (long) river in the world.

7. Because of its natural gas resources, Qatar is one of _____ _____ (rich country) in the world.

8. Chile has a _____ (diverse) climate than Ecuador, and it has _____ (extreme) climate in South America.

9. _____ (big) export from Spain is the automobile.

10. Climbing Mount Everest is one of _____ (difficult climb) in the world.

11. Rice is a _____ (important) crop for Asia than for North America.

12. Russia is _____ (large) China, but China is much _____ (populated) Russia.

2. **Comparing nouns.** Look at the picture of Greenville, a small farming community. Use *(much) more . . . than, less . . . than . . . , fewer . . . than, many more . . . than* to compare the area where you live now and Greenville. You may use the topics in the box or other topics for your comparisons.

stores
movie theaters
farms
pollution
restaurants
traffic
trees
noise

1. Greenville has _____ fewer stores than _____ my town does.

2. Greenville has _____ my town does.

3. Greenville has _____ my town does.

4. Greenville has _____ my town does.

5. My town has _____ Greenville does.

6. My town has _____ Greenville does.

7. My town has _____ Greenville does.

3. **Compare your town with Greenville using the adjectives from the box or other adjectives.**

clean	quiet	busy	wide	friendly	interesting	good	bad

1. _____

2. _____

3. _____

4. _____

5. _____

4. Use the information in the chart and write sentences of comparison using *as many . . . as* or *not as many . . . as*.

France has as many telephones as it has televisions.
Meaning: the number is the same.
Brazil doesn't have as many cell phones as France does.
Meaning: The numbers aren't the same.

Country	Official languages	Political parties	Airports	Tourists per year (million)
Thailand	4	8	111	10.8
Philippines	2	8	275	1.9
Singapore	2	9	9	7.57
India	16	25	334	2.35

(*Source*: World Factbook)

1. Thailand doesn't have _____ as many airports as _____ the Philippines does.

2. The Philippines has _____ Singapore does.

3. Thailand doesn't have _____ India does.

4. Thailand has _____ the Philippines does.

5. Singapore doesn't have _____ India does.

6. The Philippines has almost _____ Singapore does.

7. India doesn't attract _____ Thailand and Singapore do.

5. Look at the chart above. Read and circle *T* for *True* or *F* for *False*.

1. Thailand has the most official languages. T F

2. Singapore and the Philippines have the fewest official languages. T F

3. Thailand and the Philippines have almost as many political parties as Singapore does. T F

4. India has many more political parties than the other countries do. T F

5. The Philippines has more than twice as many airports as Thailand does. T F

6. India has the fewest airports. T F

7. The Philippines attracts many more tourists than Thailand does. T F

8. India attracts fewer tourists than both Singapore and Thailand do. T F

6. Look at the picture of the Parker family. Write six sentences comparing the members of the family. You may compare height, age, hair, or other features.

The Parkers

Ann Zoe Peter

The Deans

Jake
Diane

1. _Mrs. Parker's hair is much longer and curlier than her husband's._

2. _____

3. _____

4. _____

5. _____

6. _____

7. Write four sentences comparing the Parkers and the Deans. You may compare the size of the family, the number of children, and the members of the families.

1. The Parkers _____ .

2. The Parkers _____ .

3. The Deans _____ .

4. The Deans _____ .

8. Edit. Find and correct the mistake in each sentence.

      biggest
1. The ~~most big~~ country in South America is Brazil.

2. The Andes Mountains are the higher mountains in South America.

3. Most crowded country in South America is Ecuador.

4. The Galapagos Islands are the more popular destination for tourists in Ecuador.

5. Thailand is more populated then Singapore.

6. The Philippines isn't as populated India.

7. South Africa is one of the wealthiest country in Africa.

9. Three botanical gardens. Listen and complete.

1. The University of Padova has _____ one of the oldest _____ botanical gardens in the world.

2. Padova is the home of _____ medical schools.

3. The Butchart Gardens aren't _____ Padova's garden, but they attract _____.

4. _____ time to visit the Butchart Gardens is during the summer.

5. Brooklyn Botanic Garden has _____ rose gardens in the United States.

6. Brooklyn Botanic Garden has

_____

collections of Japanese cherry trees outside of Japan.

Butchart Gardens

10. Listen and complete the chart.

Garden	Year founded	Size (acres)	Admission	Summer hours	Special Feature
Butchart Gardens Victoria, Canada	1904	55	Adults: $20 Children: $1.50	9 A.M. – 10:30 P.M.	Over 100,000 tulips in spring
Brooklyn Botanic Garden, New York					
University of Padova Botanic Garden, Italy					

11. Listen and write complete answers to the questions.

1. The University of Padova's Botanic Garden was founded the earliest.

2. _____

3. _____

4. _____

5. _____

6. _____

Reading: The Biggest Blackout

On a very hot summer day in August, 2003, a power failure in Ohio started the biggest blackout North America has ever experienced. More than 100 power plants crashed, cutting off electricity in eight states from Ohio in the Midwest to New York in the northeast, and in Canada.

In Cleveland, Ohio, power went out shortly after 4:00 P.M. Elevators in tall office buildings stopped, and people walked down many flights of stairs. At least one million people lost electricity. The governor declared a state of emergency because many parts of the city had no water. Drivers drove to other cities trying to find gas for their cars because gas stations didn't have power. At the airport, planes landed safely, but all airlines cancelled flights. Many travelers had to stay at the airport. The mayor of Cleveland ordered a 9:30 P.M. curfew for teenagers 18 and under, but there were no reports of violence or looting of stores.

In Toronto, the biggest city in Ontario, the government also declared a state of emergency. Commuters got stuck in traffic when the electricity went out. At a number of busy intersections, drivers left their cars to help direct traffic. Thousands of people were stuck in the subways, and office workers walked down the stairs to get home on foot or in taxis. Flights at both Toronto and Ottawa airports could not depart for many hours. About ten million people were affected by the blackout. Like Cleveland, the local government set curfews to try to prevent looting.

New York City's Central Park became an overnight campground. Stranded visitors and city residents slept under the stars to escape the heat. About 400 subway trains stopped; subway workers and firefighters helped riders to safety. Workers had to walk miles across highways and over bridges to their homes. City buses tried to get everyone home safely.

Long lines and tired passengers crowded the three area airports as travelers had to reschedule their flights. Approximately 750 flights were affected.

New Yorkers helped each other. Drivers helped police direct traffic when traffic lights went out. Restaurants, in danger of losing thousands of dollars worth of food, gave away the food in their freezers and refrigerators. In one neighborhood, a restaurant owner took a grill outside and cooked all of the restaurant's meat, giving the neighborhood an outdoor barbecue party. In general, the city was calm. New Yorkers took advantage of the nice weather and stayed outside during the evening.

Read each statement and (circle) the correct city or cities.

1. There was a state of emergency.   Cleveland   Toronto   NYC

2. Subway riders had to escape to safety.   Cleveland   Toronto   NYC

3. Gas stations didn't have power to pump gas.   Cleveland   Toronto   NYC

4. Commuters walked home.   Cleveland   Toronto   NYC

5. Drivers directed traffic.   Cleveland   Toronto   NYC

6. People slept outside.   Cleveland   Toronto   NYC

7. Restaurants gave away food.   Cleveland   Toronto   NYC

8. The city government set curfews.   Cleveland   Toronto   NYC

5 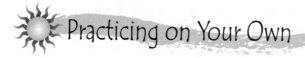 Leisure Activities

Practicing on Your Own

1. Complete the *yes/no* questions with one of the words from the box. In some questions, more than one answer is possible.

is	are	was	were	did	do	will

1. ____Did____ you play tennis last weekend?
2. _____ they going to take a vacation?
3. _____ your brother a member of the basketball team?
4. _____ you and your family go skiing next month?
5. _____ you know how to play cricket?
6. _____ they members of the volleyball team?
7. _____ your grandfather fishing with your brother today?
8. _____ you interested in stamps when you were a child?
9. _____ he a good dominoes player?
10. _____ he at the painting class last night?
11. _____ your sisters also like to sew when they were young?
12. _____ you grow flowers or vegetables in your garden?
13. _____ you and your friends go dancing next weekend?

2. Write *yes/no* questions about José and his friends. Use the clues and the correct verb tense.

1. José/play dominoes/last Saturday
   __Did José play dominoes last Saturday?__ Yes, he did.
2. they/play/every Saturday
   _____ Yes, they do.
3. José/a smart player
   _____ Yes, he is.
4. they / play / later today
   _____ No, they aren't.

3. Complete the questions with *whom/who/whose*.

> *Whose* umbrella is under the chair?
> *Who* likes sports?
> *Whom* are you writing to?
> *Who* did you call last night?
>
> *Whose* refers to possession.
> *Who* refers to the subject.
> *Whom* and *who* can both refer to the object.
> *Whom* is more formal.

Lisa

Mr. Li

Vicky, Fernando

1. _____Who_____ likes to sew?   Lisa does.

2. _____ sewing machine is she using?   Her grandmother's.

3. _____ is she making the quilt for?   For her sister.

4. _____ is playing mah-jong?   Mr. Li is.

5. _____ is he playing with?   With his father and friends.

6. _____ home are they playing at?   At Mr. Li's home.

7. _____ is dancing with Vicky?   Fernando is.

8. _____ is at the club   Their friends are.
with Vicky and Fernando?

4. Write questions using *who, whom,* or *whose* according to the information in the paragraph.

Patty likes to play card games, and she especially enjoys playing bridge. She learned how to play with three of her friends. Now they play every week. Every Saturday, they play at a different friend's home. Today, they're playing at Patty's. Patty's mother, Carla, is playing today because Patty's friend, Joanna, is sick.

1. _____ ?   Patty does.

2. _____ ?   With three friends.

3. _____ ?   Patty and her friends do.

4. _____ ?   Patty's house.

5. _____ ?   Joanna is.

5. Complete the questions using the correct expression from the box.

| How | How far | How often | How long | How much | How many |

1. _____How far_____ do you live from school?

2. _____ do you plan to study at this school?

3. _____ students are there in your class?

4. _____ do you get to school?

5. _____ did you pay for this class?

6. _____ does your class meet?

7. _____ books do you need for this class?

8. _____ will it take you to learn English?

9. _____ is it from school to your home?

10. _____ are you absent from class?

6. Complete the questions about the picture with *do, does, did,* or with a form of the verb *be.* One answer is negative.

Are you a pet owner?
What is your address?
When does this class begin?
What kind of car do you have?
Why didn't you buy a smaller one?
When did you learn how to play bridge?

Ryan   April

1. Who _____ planning a trip?   Ryan and April are.

2. What kind of trip _____ they planning?   A hiking trip.

3. Where _____ they go last year?   To Europe.

4. How long _____ the trip?   Two weeks.

5. How _____ they get from place to place? By train and on foot.

6. _____ they enjoy the trip?   No, they didn't.

7. Why _____ they enjoy the trip?   Because it rained.

8. Where _____ they going this year?   To China.

9. How long _____ they plan to stay away?   Three weeks.

10. How _____ they going to travel from   By bicycle.
    place to place?

7. Read the paragraph. Then, write questions using the information in the story. Use the simple present, present continuous, future, or past tenses.

Marco is taking a cooking course. He is single and lives with his mother and two sisters. They do everything for him—they do his laundry, and they even cook his meals. Next month, Marco is going to move out of state because of a new job. Tomorrow, Marco's going to surprise his mother and sisters with a special dinner to thank them for doing so much for him. He started a cooking course five weeks ago, and tonight is the last class. Before the course, Marco didn't know how to even boil an egg! Now, he feels much more comfortable in the kitchen. He's going to prepare his mother's favorite soup recipe, grilled steak, rice, fresh vegetables, and a delicious dessert. He's nervous about the dinner, but he's ready to surprise his family.

1. What kind of _____?

2. Who _____?

3. Whom _____?

4. Why _____?

5. What _____?

6. When _____?

7. Did _____?

8. How _____?

9. What _____?

8. Complete the tag for each question.

> They are having a nice time, aren't they?
> You don't like to fish, do you?

1. They're taking pictures,
   _____ _____?

2. They enjoy photography,
   _____ _____?

3. It isn't a warm day, _____ _____?

4. They belong to a photography club, _____ _____?

5. They aren't in the city, _____ _____?

Listening

9. Listen and write the correct tag.

1. ____aren't you?____
2. _____
3. _____
4. _____
5. _____

6. _____
7. _____
8. _____
9. _____
10. _____

10. Listen and number the correct answers from 1 to 10.

_____ I take the bus.

_____ Twelve hours a week.

_____ It was great!

___1___ $750.

_____ About three hours.

_____ About fifteen minutes on foot.

_____ Every four hours.

_____ Only three.

_____ Four days.

_____ Every morning for thirty minutes.

11. Listen to each conversation and answer the questions.

Conversation 1

1. Where are they? _____

2. What is Emma doing? _____

3. How is the weather? _____

4. Why isn't Ben going to help her? _____

Conversation 2

1. What class are the man and woman taking? _____

2. Is the man happy with his project?_____

3. What class did he take last semester?_____

4. What does he think of the woman's painting? _____

Reading: Olympic Pin Collecting and Trading

Collecting is a hobby that anyone can enjoy. Buttons and pins are two collectible items. During presidential campaigns, supporters wear buttons that support their favorite candidate's name or special slogan such as "Nixon, Now More Than Ever," which supporters for President Nixon wore in the early 70s. Protest buttons, which are buttons that express the wearer's opinion about a political cause, are also popular.

Buttons and pins can also celebrate events. One such collectible pin is a pin that celebrates the Olympic Games.

 Olympic pins are souvenirs that appear at each Olympic game. Since pins appear at every Olympic Games, many people have built large collections of pins. The pins represent individual events, the cities where the Olympics take place, and even the sponsors who help pay for the events. Each Olympic pin contains the year, the city, and the five gold rings, the symbol of the Olympic spirit. Pins are specific to the Olympic city. The summer Olympics of 2004 have pins that reflect the culture of Greece, home of the first organized Olympic Games. Every two years pin collectors have a new group of pins to collect and trade and can meet other pin collectors from around the world.

The first souvenir pins appeared at the Olympics in Stockholm, Sweden, in 1912. Today the most popular pin of those Olympics is worth $100 to $150. Like stamps, pins can increase in value if they are unusual or particularly popular. A group of valuable but hard-to-find pins are the pins from the 1940 Winter and Summer Games. Because of World War II, the games were cancelled, but the organizers produced the pins anyway.

The most popular activity for pin collectors at the Olympic Games is pin trading. One collector will try to negotiate a trade with another collector. The best situation is to make the collectors happy by trading to acquire new pins that they both want. After many years, pin collecting and trading had become so popular that by 1980, the official Olympic Pin Club met for the first time at the Lake Placid Games. The first pin trading center, a place where pin collectors could meet, opened in 1984, at the Los Angeles Summer games. In 1996 in Atlanta, Georgia, collectors traded approximately three million pins.

Scan the reading. Then, number and <u>underline</u> the answers to the questions.

1. What is a protest button?
2. What do the Olympic pins represent?
3. What three items are on every pin?
4. Why are some pins more valuable than others?
5. Why are the pins of 1940 valuable?
6. At which Olympics did pin collectors have their own place to meet trade pins?

Word forms: Complete the sentences with the correct word form.

collect	collectible	collection	collectors

1. Some people think that some pins are more _____ than others.
2. Pin _____ can meet every two years at the Olympics.
3. People also like to _____ election buttons.
4. A valuable _____ could contain pins from every Olympic event.

6 Driving

☀ Practicing on Your Own

1. **Read the rules about driving. Complete the sentences with _must_ or _must not_.**

   1. You ____must____ drive on the right side of the road in the United States.
   2. You _____ drive over the speed limit.
   3. You _____ put money in the parking meters.
   4. You _____ park illegally.
   5. Drivers _____ drive too closely to the car in front of them.
   6. Drivers _____ pass a loading school bus.
   7. Drivers _____ use their headlights at night.
   8. When young drivers have their permits, they _____ drive with a licensed driver.

2. **Read the sentences about students at your school. Then write sentences using modals from the box.**

have to has to	had to didn't have to	doesn't have to don't have to

   1. Students ____have to____ buy books.
   2. I ____didn't have to____ buy my books for this class.
   3. Students _____ wait in long lines to register for class.
   4. I _____ wait in a long line when I registered.
   5. Students with cars _____ get parking permits.
   6. I _____ get a parking permit.
   7. New students _____ attend an orientation.
   8. I _____ attend an orientation.
   9. All ESL students _____ take a placement test.
   10. I _____ take a placement test.
   11. A typical student _____ come to school five days a week.
   12. I _____ come to school Monday to Friday.
   13. A typical student _____ use a dictionary.
   14. I _____ buy a dictionary for this class.

3. Write sentences for each question. Use *can* or *can't* in your answer.

a. What can students do if they speak English fluently?

1. _They can speak to people in stores easily._

2. _____

3. _____

b. What can't students do if they can't read and write English?

1. _____

2. _____

3. _____

c. Write three things that you can do in English.

1. _____

2. _____

3. _____

4. Read each situation. Give advice using *should* or *shouldn't*.

1. Tatyana is happy about her new job, but she's worried about transportation. She doesn't have enough money to buy a new car. What should she do?

   She _____

2. Mrs. Paz is ninety years old. She's in very good health for her age, but her family doesn't want her to drive anymore. Mrs. Paz doesn't want to give up her car. What should her family do?

   _____

3. Richard wants to join the school soccer team, but he's very thin. He wants to gain some weight and some muscle, but he wants to do it safely. What should he do?

   _____

4. Fernando is fifteen years old. He wants to buy a new CD, but his parents won't give him any more money for CDs. What should he do?

   _____

5. Marie's son, Pierre, loves to play video games. It's his favorite activity, but Marie wants him to get some exercise and fresh air. What should she do?

   _____

5. Read each sign and write a warning. Use *had better* or *had better not*.

No food or drinks in the computer lab	1. <u>That student had better finish his coffee before he goes</u> <u>into the lab.</u>
No lifeguard on duty at Sandy Lane Beach	2. We _____ .
Hospital Zone No Cell Phones	3. Visitors _____ .
Caution! Hard Hat Area	4. Workers _____ .
No pets allowed in this building	5. Residents _____ .
Microwave Warning No metal utensils	6. You _____ .

6. Rewrite each sentence using one of the modals from the box. Some sentences are negative.

> have to   had to   must   had better   should   can

1. It is necessary for drivers to stop at a red light.

   Drivers _____ .

2. It is against the rules for you to use a cell phone here.

   You _____ .

3. It is not necessary for the mechanic to change the oil today.

   My mechanic _____ .

4. It is a good idea for us to leave early today.

   We _____ .

5. She warned her son to study harder.

   Mother: You _____.

6. Victoria has the ability to speak Spanish and Portuguese.

   She _____.

7. Do not leave your children alone in the car.

   I _____.

8. It is not a good idea to drive when you're tired.

   I _____.

9. It is the rule for all students to buy their books.

   I _____.

10. It was necessary for me to fill out an application to come to this class.

    All students _____.

11. It is not necessary for me to buy a computer for this class.

    I _____.

12. It is a requirement for all students to have a hepatitis B vaccine.

    I _____.

13. It is a bad idea to copy someone else's homework.

    You _____.

7. Edit. Find and correct each mistake.

                    to

1. All students have ∧ do homework.

2. You must to have two forms of identification.

3. You shouldn't drinking hot beverages while driving.

4. We better leave early.

5. She can't plays a musical instrument.

6. Our neighbors have better turn down their stereo.

7. Bianca didn't had to buy new clothes when she came to this country.

8. Felicia should practices before she takes her road test.

8. Listen to people talk about driving. Complete with *can* or *can't*.

1. I _____ a manual transmission.

2. He _____ in the city.

3. Vehicles _____ on the right.

4. I _____ a large vehicle.

5. She _____ an SUV.

6. The children _____ videos in the back seat.

7. We _____ over 25 miles per hour in this area.

8. She _____ her license in two months.

9. He _____ the car without his parents' permission.

10. They _____ in a car without car seats.

9. Listen and complete the sentences about Leo's new job. Use *must* or *must not* and an appropriate verb.

1. Leo _____ his uniform outside of work.

2. Leo _____ into his uniform in the locker room.

3. He _____ a name tag.

4. He _____ a time clock.

5. He _____ personal calls during company time.

6. He _____ more than thirty minutes for lunch.

7. He _____ overtime in the fall.

8. The company _____ double time to all employees who work overtime more than once a week.

10. Listen and write a suggestion for each person. Use *should* or *shouldn't*.

1. He _____.

2. He _____.

3. She _____.

4. She _____.

5. He _____.

6. She _____.

A driver's responsibility is to operate a vehicle safely and to pay attention to the road and the other vehicles. Most people think about cell phones when they think about distractions for drivers because cell phones have received the most attention. There are many other distractions that can make a driver lose control and cause an accident.

Because there are many drive-up restaurants, drivers eat more often in their cars. According to an insurance company report, eating while driving causes more accidents in the morning, when people are on their way to work. If you have to eat in your car, avoid hot liquids like coffee and messy foods like hamburgers and sandwiches. You should drink out of a closed container, or take a bite when you come to a full stop.

Other passengers can distract a driver, too. According to AAA, the American Automobile Association, babies distract drivers more than adult passengers do. When babies are in the car, drivers tend to turn around and comfort the babies if they start to cry. If you have babies or young children in your car, you should not feed, dress, or play with them while you are driving.

Cars have radios, cassette players, CD players, lights, air conditioners, and heaters. Each item has a control dial or knob that requires some attention, but you should not make adjustments, like changing your CD, while you are driving. In fact, ten states already have warnings about radios in their driver's manuals. You should make adjustments in your car before you leave home.

Another distraction can be stress. Drivers who have arguments with family members at home or with someone at work will get into their cars angry. They may drive more aggressively or be distracted by thinking about their argument. Sometimes an argument in the car can cause a driver to stop paying attention to the road. If you are feeling very upset or angry, you should try to relax before you get into your car. If you are driving on a busy road and something makes you so upset that you cannot concentrate on driving, you should pull over to the side of the road. Take a moment to calm down before you continue and you will have a much safer trip.

Read and (circle) T for *True* or F for *False*.

1.	Cell phones distract drivers from the road.	T	F
2.	More people drive and eat at night than in the morning.	T	F
3.	You should never drink soda in the car.	T	F
4.	Hot liquids are dangerous to drink while driving.	T	F
5.	Babies distract drivers more than adults do.	T	F
6.	Drivers should not feed their babies in the car.	T	F
7.	All states have warnings about radios in their driver's manuals.	T	F
8.	Drivers should adjust their radios before they start the car.	T	F
9.	You should not drive when you are very angry.	T	F

7 Sports

Practicing on Your Own

1. Circle *for* or *since*.

1. Martin has been playing basketball **for / since** two hours.
2. Jose has been riding a bicycle **for / since** he was five years old.
3. The family has been camping **for / since** three days.
4. I have been swimming **for / since** a little while.
5. Jean and Dennis have been watching that movie **for / since** 3:00.
6. He's been at that company **for / since** six years.
7. They've been saving for retirement **for / since** 1990.
8. Alberto has been dating Teresa **for / since** September.
9. Lynn and Mike have been sailing **for / since** three weeks.
10. We've been driving **for / since** the sun came up.
11. The forest rangers have been looking for the lost hiker **for / since** Monday.

2. Match these sentence halves. Then, complete the sentences below.

_d_ 1. He's on a low-sodium diet,
___ 2. He's trying out for the team,
___ 3. He lost his license,
___ 4. He broke his arm,
___ 5. He failed his test,
___ 6. His girlfriend left him,
___ 7. He has allergies,

a. so he's been taking the bus to work.
b. so he's been very lonely.
c. so his girlfriend has been typing all his papers.
d. so he has been using less salt.
e. so he's been taking antihistamines.
f. so he's been working out every day.
g. so he's been studying very hard.

8. She lost her job, so _____.
9. They want to buy a house, so _____.
10. He wants to get a promotion, so _____.
11. She would like to play the piano, so _____.
12. He has a bad back, so _____.

3. Write questions and answers about the people in Café Click. Use *How long*.

1. How long have Sam and Yolanda been sitting in the café?

   They've been sitting there for an hour.

2. How long has Carson _____?

   _____

3. How long _____?

   _____

4. How long _____?

   _____

5. How long _____?

   _____

6. How long _____?

   _____

7. How long _____?

   _____

4. Complete these sentences about the pictures. Use the cues.

play/begin

1. They _____are playing_____ baseball now.
2. They _____began_____ to play at 4:00.
3. They ____have been playing____ baseball for two hours.

run

4. They _____ in the park now.
5. They _____ since 10:00.
6. They _____ in the park yesterday, too.

work out/arrive

7. Sherri _____ at the gym three days a week.
8. She _____ at the gym an hour ago.
9. She _____ for an hour.
10. She _____ at the gym again tomorrow.

clean

11. Sherri _____ her house now.
12. She _____ her house every Friday.
13. She _____ since breakfast.

talk/call

14. Sherri _____ with her sister now.
15. They _____ about Sherri's new job.
16. Her sister _____ her an hour ago.
17. They _____ for a long time.

wash/go

18. Sherri only _____ her car once a month.
19. She _____ her car now.
20. She _____ her car for thirty minutes.
21. Next time, she _____ to the car wash.

5. Complete these conversations.

A: Excuse me. ____Is____ this the bus to Fairfield?

B: Yes, it is.

A: What time _____?

B: The next bus is at 5:00.

A: It's 5:10. How long _____?

B: I've been waiting for twenty minutes. The bus is late.

A: What happened?

B: I _____ my keys in my car.

A: How long _____ to open the door?

B: For about an hour.

A: It's time to call a locksmith.

A: How _____?

B: I fell down the stairs.

A: _____

B: No, I can't write.

A: _____

B: No, it doesn't hurt anymore.

A: What _____?

B: He robbed a bank.

A: How long _____?

B: He's been in jail for almost a year.

A: _____

B: He's going to get out next month.

A: Where _____?

B: I'm on Route 1. I'm stuck in traffic.

A: How long _____?

B: I've been sitting in traffic for an hour.

A: When _____?

B: I'm going to call my boss in a minute.

6. **Listen to these statements about sports. Is the action continuing or is the action finished?**

	The action is continuing.	The action is finished.		The action is continuing.	The action is finished.
1.	☐	☑	7.	☐	☐
2.	☐	☐	8.	☐	☐
3.	☐	☐	9.	☐	☐
4.	☐	☐	10.	☐	☐
5.	☐	☐	11.	☐	☐
6.	☐	☐	12.	☐	☐

7. **Listen to these short conversations. Circle the true information.**

1. a. The team has been winning more games.
   b. The team hasn't been doing very well.
2. a. She's been losing weight.
   b. She's been gaining weight.
3. a. Larry has been running two miles a day.
   b. Larry hasn't been running.
4. a. He's been using the gym a lot.
   b. He hasn't been using the gym very often.
5. a. She's been doing well in school.
   b. She hasn't been doing well in school.
6. a. She's been going out with David for two years.
   b. She's been going out with someone new.

8. **Listen to the information about Stan and look at the time line. Then, answer each question in a complete sentence.**

Taxi driver New York	Bus driver San Francisco	Truck driver Boston
1990	1995	2000

1. _____
2. _____
3. _____
4. _____
5. _____
6. _____
7. _____

Vocabulary. Match the word with its meaning. Read the article. Then, complete the sentences below the article with a word from the list.

__b__ **1.** to attract   **a.** a person who served in the military

____ **2.** a disability   **b.** to interest

____ **3.** a veteran   **c.** to take part in a sports event

____ **4.** an injury   **d.** a person who watches a sports event

____ **5.** to compete   **e.** a physical problem from birth or from an accident

____ **6.** a limb   **f.** damage or hurt, e.g., a bad back or a broken leg

____ **7.** to evaluate   **g.** an arm or a leg

____ **8.** a spectator   **h.** to judge

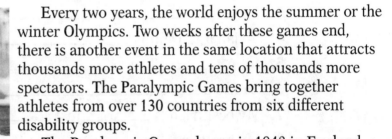

Every two years, the world enjoys the summer or the winter Olympics. Two weeks after these games end, there is another event in the same location that attracts thousands more athletes and tens of thousands more spectators. The Paralympic Games bring together athletes from over 130 countries from six different disability groups.

The Paralympic Games began in 1948 in England. Sir Ludwig Guttman organized a sports competition for veterans of World War II who had suffered spinal cord injuries. These athletes in wheelchairs competed again four years later, with athletes from the Netherlands joining the games. As more people learned about the games, athletes from more countries began to enter the different events and more disability classes were added.

Today, athletes from six different disability classes compete in the Paralympics. Many athletes are in wheelchairs; some have suffered spinal injuries or are missing a limb. Blind athletes compete with a sighted companion. Other classes include athletes with polio, spina bifida, or cerebral palsy. Athletes are carefully evaluated so that they compete with individuals of similar abilities.

There are nineteen sports in the Summer Paralympics, including swimming, table tennis, cycling, and powerlifting. Athletics, one of the most popular events, includes running, throwing, and wheelchair competitions. Team sports such as wheelchair basketball, wheelchair tennis, and wheelchair rugby attract thousands of spectators.

The popularity of the Paralympic Games has been growing. More than 4,000 athletes have been practicing to compete in the upcoming games. The Paralympic website www.paralympic.org provides information on the location of the next Paralympic Games and the history of this great sports competition.

1. Each athlete competes with a _____, such as loss of a limb.

2. The Paralympics Games _____ thousands of spectators.

3. One of the athletes was a _____ of the Gulf War.

4. Another athlete suffered a back _____ in a car accident.

5. Judges _____ the ability of each athlete.

Changes

Practicing on Your Own

1. Complete these sentences. Write the verb in the present perfect.

1. My parents ___have___ just ___returned___ (return) from a Caribbean cruise.
2. Silvia _____ (open) a travel agency.
3. Moses _____ (meet) a wonderful woman.
4. Vivian and Dennis _____ (be) married since 2000.
5. John _____ just _____ (buy) a sports car
6. Laurie _____ (feel–negative) well lately.
7. My best friends _____ just _____ (have) twins.
8. My brother _____ (grow) a beard.
9. Danny and Vanessa _____ (be) divorced for six months.
10. Jack _____ (graduate-negative) from college yet.
11. Carlos and Luisa _____ (fall) in love.
12. My daughter _____ (join) the navy.
13. My uncle _____ just _____ (get) his pilot's license.
14. Paul _____ (attend) college part time for six years.
15. My father is 70, but he _____ (retire-negative) yet.
16. My brother is in China. I _____ (see-negative) him since 1990.
17. We _____ (visit) every country in Europe.
18. Joseph _____ (change) jobs recently.
19. Rita _____ (move) to Detroit.

2. Complete these sentences. Use the negative verb form.

1. I used to see her every day, but I ___haven't seen___ her since she started her new job.
2. They used to eat at La Casita every Friday night, but they _____ _____ there since Claudia got sick.
3. She used to walk in the park every day, but she _____ in the park since she broke her foot.

4. He used to fail all of his tests, but he _____ a test since he got a private tutor.

5. He used to drive over the speed limit, but _____ over the speed limit since he got a ticket.

6. She used to stop at the donut shop every day, but she _____ at the donut shop since she started her diet.

7. He used to take the bus to work every day, but he _____ the bus since he bought a car.

8. She used to visit Portugal every summer, but she _____ Portugal since her parents moved to the United States.

3. Describe the changes you see in these pictures using the present perfect. The first picture shows Debbie ten years ago. The second picture shows Debbie now.

1. <u>She's become the vice president of the company.</u>

2. _____

3. _____

4. _____

5. _____

6. _____

7. _____

4. Tense contrast. Complete these sentences about the pictures using the correct form of the verb.

1. Paul _____**goes**_____ (go) fishing every weekend.

2. Paul _____ (fish) in the river now.

3. He _____ (catch) any fish yet.

4. Ruth _____ just _____ (arrive) at work.

5. She _____ (greet) her co-workers.

6. She _____ (sit) down at her desk yet.

7. These two men _____ just _____ an (have) accident.

8. They _____ already _____ (call) the police.

9. The police _____ (arrive) yet.

10. Pat _____ (take) the bus to work every day.

11. Pat _____ (get) to the bus stop thirty minutes ago.

12. The bus _____ (come) yet.

13. Jen _____ (wake) up at 6:45 every morning.

14. Her alarm clock _____ (ring) fifteen minutes ago.

15. She _____ (get) out of bed yet.

5. What have you done this year? What haven't you done this year? Use the cues and write about each activity using *already* or *yet*.

1. (pay my car insurance) <u>I've already paid my car insurance.</u>

2. (miss a class) <u>I haven't missed a class yet.</u>

3. (take a vacation) _____

4. (have a physical) _____

5. (file my income taxes) _____

6. (fail an exam) _____

7. (celebrate my birthday) _____

8. (go to the emergency room) _____

9. (buy a digital camera) _____

10. (get a parking ticket) _____

Listening

6. **There is a hurricane warning in Florida. Listen to these ten sentences about the picture. Write the six sentences that are true.**

1. <u>The wind has begun to blow.</u>

2. _____

3. _____

4. _____

5. _____

6. _____

7. Listen to the questions. Write the answers in the correct tense—present perfect or past.

1. Yes, I _____ it yesterday.
2. No, I _____ it yet.
3. Yes, it _____ at 10:00.
4. Yes, I _____ it in July.
5. Yes, I _____ already.
6. Yes, he _____ it in the car.
7. No, I _____ it yet.
8. Yes, I _____ him already.
9. No, she _____ .
10. Yes, it _____ at 3:00.
11. Yes, I _____ there last night.
12. Yes, I _____ to her already.

8. Luisa is expecting a baby in three weeks. Listen to the preparations for the new baby. Check *Completed* or *Not completed*. Then, write seven sentences about the information in the chart using *already* or *yet*.

Preparations	Completed	Not completed
Choose a boy's name		
Choose a girl's name		
Paint the baby's room		
Order the furniture		
Buy a car seat		
Take childbirth classes		
Buy a digital camera		
Stop working		
Pack her suitcase		

1. Luisa and Alberto have already chosen a boy's name.
2. _____
3. _____
4. _____
5. _____
6. _____
7. _____
8. _____

Reading: Automobile Safety Features

bumpers

When families shop for new cars, safety features are an important consideration. Many of these features, such as seat belts, are standard in all cars. In the past ten years, auto makers have developed a number of new safety systems to **prevent** accidents. Some are now available in cars, while others are still in the planning **stages**.

The makers of most new cars have installed front air bags for the driver and the passenger and many manufacturers also offer side air bags.

Many car manufacturers offer telematics systems as an **option**. These expensive services use global positioning satellite technology. If you are lost, the service will give you directions. If you are in an accident, the service will call the police. If you need an ambulance, the service can call for emergency help and give your location.

Car bumpers have also changed. In the past, a light **impact** would cause thousands of dollars of damage. Today, a five-mile-an-hour crash will not seriously damage a car. Drivers may need to **replace** the plastic bumpers, but there is little **damage** to the car body.

A few manufacturers have installed front and rear end sensing technology. This system makes a warning sound if the car is within six feet of a person, vehicle, or other object. For example, it can **alert** the driver to a person walking behind the car or a child playing in the driveway.

Car manufacturers are also working to develop a "wandering" **detection system**. Drivers on highways and freeways sometimes become sleepy or distracted. Cameras in the car check the position of the car. If the car seems to be traveling too much to the left or the right of the center of the lane, a warning sound goes off.

Auto makers continue to develop new safety systems. Many are still in the planning stages and will not be available for several years.

Find the information about car safety features.

1. Underline the six safety features described in this article.

2. I have the following safety features on my car: _____

   _____

3. Which feature is not yet available? _____

Match these words from the reading with their definitions.

__e__ 1. to prevent   **a.** an additional feature, not a standard feature

____ 2. a stage   **b.** a crash or collision

____ 3. an impact   **c.** a system which warns of danger

____ 4. to replace   **d.** to warn about a problem

____ 5. damage   **e.** to avoid, to stop from happening

____ 6. an option   **f.** to put in a new part

____ 7. to alert   **g.** a step in a process

____ 8. detection system   **h.** injury to a person or a thing

9 Job Performance

1. Ask and answer questions about these pictures.

1. What's he doing?
   He's making a pizza.

2. How long has he been making pizzas?
   He's been making pizzas for three hours.

3. How many pizzas has he made so far?
   He's made 30 pizzas so far.

1. What's he doing?
   _____.

2. How long has he been selling hot dogs?
   _____

3. How many hot dogs has he sold?
   _____

1. What _____?
   _____

2. How long _____?
   _____

3. How many _____?
   _____

1. What _____?
   _____.

2. How long _____?
   _____.

3. How many _____?
   _____.

2. Write the words in these sentences in the correct order.

1. arrived / Mark / late / has / seldom / for / work
   Mark has seldom arrived late for work.

2. without / He / missed / notice / never / has / work
   _____

3. five times / put in / He / overtime / this month / has
   _____

4. received / just / He / promotion / has / a
   _____

5. a / few / trained / employees / He / has / new / times
   _____

6. managed / time / He / the / time / to / office / from / has
   _____

7. recently / completed / He / a / program / has / training
   _____

3. Answer these questions about yourself. Use a time expression or an adverb of frequency.

1. Have you ever had a job interview in English?
   _____

2. Have you ever arrived at work late?
   _____

3. Have you ever overslept?
   _____

4. Have you ever stayed up all night?
   _____

5. Have you ever lost your house keys?
   _____

6. Have you ever sent someone flowers?
   _____

4. Max. Answer the questions about the time line.

Marino's Restaurant

Graduated from high school	Bus boy $6.00 an hour	Waiter $4.00 + tips	Cook $15.00 an hour
2000	2001	2003	

1. When did Max graduate from high school?

   _____

2. When did Max begin to work at Marino's?

   _____

3. How long has he been working at Marino's?

   _____

4. How much did he earn as a busboy?

   _____

5. Did he receive tips as a waiter?

   _____

6. How long has he been a cook?

   _____

7. Has his salary increased since he began at Marino's?

   _____

5. Complete these conversations. Use the correct tense of the verb.

Conversation 1

Manager: _____ Has _____ our order for new parts

   _____ arrived _____ (arrive) yet?

Worker: No, it _____.

Manager: When _____ we _____
   (place) the order?

Worker: We _____ (place) it last Monday.

Manager: _____ you _____ (check)
   on the order lately?

Worker: I _____ (call) them twice so far. It

   _____ (arrive) this afternoon.

Conversation 2

Worker 1: I _____ (receive) two raises this year so far.

Worker 2: Two! I _____ (receive–negative) any yet!

Worker 1: How many new clients _____ you _____ (get) for the company this month?

Worker 2: One.

Worker 1: I _____ (got) twelve so far.

Conversation 3

Boss: That was Mrs. Jackson on the phone. She _____ (receive–negative) her flower order yet.

Worker 1: I _____ (complete) the order this morning and I (put) _____ it on the delivery truck.

Boss: I _____ (call) Mrs. Jackson and tell her to expect her order soon.

Conversation 4

Student: How long _____ (teach) at this school, Mrs. Meng?

Teacher: I _____ (teach) here for twenty years.

Student: How many days _____ (miss)?

Teacher: I _____ (miss/never) a day of work.

Student: Never?

Teacher: Never. And how about you, Tatyana? How many days _____ _____ (be) absent this year so far?

Student: Seven.

Conversation 5

Laura: Congratulations! You _____ finally _____ (finish) nursing school. What _____ (be) your plans?

Marie: I _____ (apply) to three different hospitals and they all _____ (offer) me jobs.

Laura: Which one _____ (accept)?

Marie: I think I _____ (take) the job in the emergency room at Mercy Hospital.

6. Listen to these sentences about work. Is the action or job finished? Circle Finished or Not finished.

1. (Finished)   Not finished
2. Finished   Not finished
3. Finished   Not finished
4. Finished   Not finished
5. Finished   Not finished

6. Finished   Not finished
7. Finished   Not finished
8. Finished   Not finished
9. Finished   Not finished
10. Finished   Not finished

7. Listen to each sentence. Then, circle the sentence with the same meaning.

1. a. Roberto worked at Ace Electronics for three years.
   b. Roberto has worked at Ace Electronics for three years.
2. a. Sylvia delivered 50 packages.
   b. Sylvia has delivered 50 packages so far.
3. a. Susan has taught for more than 20 years.
   b. Susan taught for more than 20 years.
4. a. Kenia changed her major twice.
   b. Kenia has changed her major twice.
5. a. Cesar took more than 300 photos at the wedding.
   b. Cesar has taken more than 300 photos at the wedding.
6. a. They won 80 games this season.
   b. They have won 80 games this season.
7. a. Laura reviewed 25 loans.
   b. Laura has reviewed 25 loans
8. a. Tony only saw six customers.
   b. Tony has only seen six customers.

8. Look at the time line and listen to Amy's job history. Answer each question in a complete sentence.

Shoes Shoes Plus	Appliances Best Appliances	Cars Car City	Insurance Samson Insurance
1995	1998	2000	2004

1. _____
2. _____
3. _____
4. _____

5. _____

6. _____

7. _____

☀ Reading: Franchises

Carol's mother was a wonderful baker. Everyone loved her cookies—chocolate chip, peanut butter, sugar cookies, and more. In 1995, when Carol decided to start a small business, her mother was happy to share her secret recipes. Mom's Cookies offered seven kinds of rich, delicious cookies. Soon, there were long lines of customers at the counter.

In 1998, Carol opened two more stores in nearby towns, and both stores were soon making a profit. Seeing her success, several business people asked Carol if they could also open a Mom's Cookies in their towns. Carol decided to franchise the business. For an initial payment of $25,000, people could use the name of her store, her business system, her suppliers, and her cookie recipes. Carol also would receive 10 percent of each store's profits. In the past five years, ten more Mom's Cookies stores have opened. Nine have been profitable; one has failed.

There are hundreds of franchise opportunities in every kind of business, such as pet services, gyms, fast-food restaurants, pest control, photography services, printing, tanning salons, and so on. According to the International Franchise Association, there were over 320,000 franchised small businesses in the United States in 2000 and many more thousands throughout the world. The initial franchise fee is typically about $30,000, but some well-known companies can charge $500,000 or more. The franchise fee does not include the equipment, real estate costs, supplies, or employees.

People interested in operating a franchise should look at several franchise opportunities and talk with current franchise owners. Some franchise companies help new owners develop a business plan. Most franchise companies offer support and training since they want their sales and services to expand and succeed. However, there are some dishonest franchises that do not live up to their promises. Research the company carefully and be sure to work with a lawyer.

Circle *T* for *True* or *F* for *False*.

1. It is easy to start a business.	T	F
2. Mom's Cookies is an example of a franchise company.	T	F
3. It can be very expensive to buy a franchise.	T	F
4. Everyone who buys a franchise makes money.	T	F
5. The franchise fee includes all the equipment a business will need.	T	F
6. Every franchise company offers a training program.	T	F
7. All franchise companies are honest.	T	F

10 Regrets and Possibilities

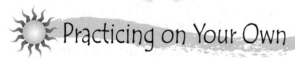

Practicing on Your Own

1. Look at each picture and complete the sentences. Use *should have* or *shouldn't have* and the verb in parentheses. Some of the sentences are negative.

1. Alan's doctor told him to cut down on fatty foods, but he didn't. Yesterday he went to his favorite restaurant and ate all of his favorite foods. Now, he feels terrible.
   a. Alan ___shouldn't have eaten___ two hamburgers. (eat)
   b. He ___should have eaten___ something healthier with less fat. (eat)

2. Chris is looking for a cheap flight for this weekend, but all of the cheap flights are full.
   a. Chris _____ his reservation earlier. (make)
   b. He _____ so long to make his reservation. (wait)

3. Noemi worked late every night this week and got very little sleep. Today, she had to come home early because she had a high fever.
   a. Noemi _____ so many hours. (work)
   b. She _____ home when she began to feel ill. (come)

4. Angela likes dogs, but when she touched the man's dog, it bit her.
   a. Angela _____ the dog. (touch)
   b. She _____ to the owner before she touched the dog. (speak)

5. Andrew left his keys in his car and went back into his house. When he came out, someone was driving his car away.
   a. Andrew _____ the keys in the ignition. (leave)
   b. He _____ more careful with his car. (be)

2. **Read each situation. Answer each question with a possibility for each situation. Use *may have*, *might have*, or *could have*. You may also use the negative form.**

1. Manny has a good job in an accounting office, but he isn't happy. What he really likes is taking care of animals.

   a. Why did he become an accountant?

   He might have wanted a job with regular hours.

   b. Why didn't he become a veterinarian?

   _____

2. Marcela works in a department store as a cashier. When her boss had to call in sick, Marcela's co-worker, Jan, volunteered to take the boss's place. Now, Jan has a promotion and is Marcela's boss.

   a. Why didn't Marcela volunteer to take over?

   _____

   b. How did Marcela feel when she heard about Jan's promotion?

   _____

3. Tom and Jessie were planning to go to see the latest Bond movie. They left at 8:30, but they're already back. It's only 9:15.

   a. What happened?

   _____

   b. Why didn't they do something else?

   _____

4. Rasheed has just come back from a vacation in Europe. He can't stop talking about his trip, and now he wants to study Italian.

   a. Why is Rasheed always talking about his trip?

   _____

   b. Why does he want to study Italian?

   _____

5. Daniela went to the Department of Motor Vehicles to renew her driver's license, but she couldn't do it. She didn't have any picture identification. What could she have used for identification?

   a. _____

   b. _____

3. **Possibilities and deductions.** Read the information and write one possibility. Use *may have, might have,* or *could have.* Then, read the additional information and write a deduction.

1. You and your friends planned to meet at 10:30. It is 10:50 now, and one of your friends still hasn't arrived.

   a. She _might have forgotten about it_____.

   Additional information: Your friend said that she had to return some tapes to the video store.

   b. She _must have gone to the video store first_____.

2. Susan called an office for information at 3:00 P.M., but she only heard an answering machine.

   a. The office _____.

   Additional information: It's the day before a national holiday weekend.

   b. The office _____.

3. The couple next to you at the restaurant was making a lot of noise. The woman was crying.

   a. They _____.

   Additional information: The man was holding a small jewelry box.

   b. He _____.

4. Kelly and her boyfriend, Scott, go everywhere together, but Kelly came to her sister's wedding alone.

   a. Kelly _____.

   Additional information: Scott is a lawyer and makes frequent business trips.

   b. Scott _____.

4. **Complete the sentences with the correct form of one of the adjectives from the box.**

bored	boring	exhausted	exhausting	interested	interesting
confused	confusing	challenged	challenging	frustrated	frustrating
excited	exciting	surprised	surprising	frightened	frightening

1. The first day of school is _exciting_____.

2. English spelling can be _____.

3. I like horror movies, but they are _____.

4. Al didn't study for the exam, so he was _____ at his good grade.

5. After Tad worked ten hours overtime, he felt _____.

6. Working as a waitress is very _____.

7. The art students were very _____ in the new art exhibit.

8. The exam was so _____ that only a few students could pass it.

5. Complete the sentences with the appropriate adjective form. Use the -ing or -ed form of one of the verbs from the box.

annoy	bore	distract	embarrass	relax	worry

1. The movie was so _____boring_____ that we didn't stay to watch the ending.

2. The soccer team was so _____ about the next game that they didn't have a good practice.

3. The scenery and the music were so _____ that I fell asleep at the concert.

4. The construction noise was so _____ that we had to leave the restaurant.

5. The driver was so _____ by the beautiful woman that he crashed into the car in front of him.

6. Dave's poor dancing was so _____ that his wife walked away from him.

6. Complete the conversation with *must have* and an appropriate adjective. Use the -ing or -ed form.

1. **A:** My grandmother won the lottery!
   B: She _must have been very excited_____.

2. **A:** Someone broke into my car last week.
   B: You _____.

3. **A:** I finally found my keys after looking for two hours.
   B: You _____.

4. **A:** When the hurricane hit, I was at home by myself.
   B: That _____.

5. **A:** I couldn't sleep last night. The neighbor's dog was barking all night.
   B: That _____.

6. **A:** My parents got divorced when I was a senior in high school.
   B: That _____.

7. **A:** After one month, my grandfather finally came home from the hospital last Saturday.
   B: Your family _____.

7. Listen and complete the sentences.

1. You _____ your coat.

2. I _____ on my phone.

3. He _____ that flight.

4. They _____ the bus.

5. She _____ a taxi.

6. It _____ on time.

7. She _____ the phone.

8. They _____ it at home on the table.

9. He _____ the sign for the exit.

10. She _____ not to come with us.

8. Listen and circle the correct answers.

1. **a.** He doesn't like his job. **b.** He likes his job.

2. **a.** He lives in a warm climate. **b.** He lives in a cold climate.

3. **a.** Her car is too small. **b.** Her car is too big.

4. **a.** He paid the bills late. **b.** He paid the bills on time.

5. **a.** She was late for an appointment. **b.** She was too early for the appointment.

6. **a.** He received a speeding ticket. **b.** He received a parking ticket.

7. **a.** She listened to her brother's advice. **b.** She didn't listen to her brother's advice.

8. **a.** She can't find her purse. **b.** She found her purse.

9. **a.** He is still hungry. **b.** He ate too much.

10. **a.** She got lost. **b.** She found the address easily.

Reading: A Strange Package

crate—a wooden box used for shipping

On September 10, 2003 an unusual package arrived at Mr. and Mrs. McKinley's front door. It was a large wooden crate, containing their son, Charles. Charles had shipped himself from New York City to his parents' home in Dallas, Texas. Instead of taking normal transportation, such as an airplane or train, Charles McKinley traveled in the bottom of a number of cargo planes.

Charles worked as a shipping clerk at a warehouse in New York. He reported that he was homesick and wanted to visit his parents in Texas. He worked for a warehouse and decided to use his experience with the shipping business to get a cheap ride back home. With the help of friends, he fit himself, his computer, and some clothes into a crate and waited for a delivery company to pick up his crate.

A delivery company picked up his crate and delivered the crate to JFK Airport in Queens, New York. The company thought that the crate was packed with computer monitors. No one knew what was really inside of the crate. At the airport, a truck took the crate to Newark, New Jersey, and put it on a cargo plane.

The crate was very uncomfortable, and Charles felt "scared and nervous" according to news reports. Unfortunately, the crate did not have a direct flight. The crate went from New Jersey, north to Buffalo, New York, and southwest to Fort Wayne, Indiana. Meanwhile, Charles used his cell phone to call a delivery company to pick up his crate in Dallas. Finally, after a change of planes, the crate arrived at the Dallas/Fort Worth International Airport. Another truck picked up the crate and drove the fourteen miles to the home of Charles's parents.

Everything was fine until the delivery man saw Charles hiding inside the crate. Then, Charles kicked down part of the crate, got out, and walked to the house. Charles's mother was shocked when she saw her son. The delivery man was scared and called the police. Charles was soon arrested for stowing away on a plane.

Do you agree or disagree? Read the passage and (circle) your opinion.

1. He must have been very homesick.   I agree.   I disagree.

2. His friends shouldn't have helped him.   I agree.   I disagree.

3. He should have waited until a cheap flight was available.   I agree.   I disagree.

4. He should have saved some money so that he could travel a normal way. I agree.   I disagree.

5. His parents should have given him money.   I agree.   I disagree.

6. The police shouldn't have arrested him.   I agree.   I disagree.

7. His boss should fire him.   I agree.   I disagree.

8. He should not work for any more delivery companies.   I agree.   I disagree.

11 Let's Get Organized

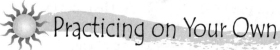

Practicing on Your Own

1. Answer the questions about each picture. Use an infinitive in each answer.

1. What does he plan to do?
<u>He plans to organize his desk.</u>

2. Where would she like to go on vacation?

_____

3. How many fish does he expect to catch?

_____

4. What does he hope to win?

_____

5. What did she agree to do?

_____

6. What do they love to do on the weekends?

_____

7. She's too tired to cook. What did she decide to order?

_____

8. What does he want to do?

_____

2. Use a verb from the box and write a statement with the advice each of these people is giving. Use an infinitive in each sentence.

advise	encourage	permit	tell
allow	expect	remind	urge
ask	forbid	require	warn

1. teacher–students (buy a dictionary)

   The teacher reminded the students to buy a dictionary.

2. doctor–patient (go on a low-fat diet)

   _____

3. parent–child (wear his bicycle helmet)

   _____

4. landlord–tenant (pay the rent on time)

   _____

5. manager–employees (wear their name tags)

   _____

6. employees–boss (provide health care benefits)

   _____

7. father–son (drive the family car)

   _____

8. mother–daughter (dye her hair purple)

   _____

9. police officer–driver (wear her seatbelt)

   _____

10. political candidate–his supporters (register to vote)

    _____

11. pilot–passengers (fasten their seatbelts)

    _____

12. security officer–passenger–show him some identification

    _____

3. **Rewrite each sentence using the verb in parentheses. Use an infinitive after the verb.**

1. Steve said, "A thousand dollars for that camera? I don't have that kind of money." (can't afford)

   Steve can't afford to buy that camera.

2. Monica said, "Jack, can you drive me to the airport?" (ask)

   Monica asked Jack to drive her to the airport.

3. Henry said, "Maria, let's go out for dinner tonight." (invite)

   _____

4. Sam said, "It's raining and my umbrella is at home!" (forget)

   _____

5. Irina said, "Don't worry. I'll study hard." (promise)

   _____

6. Liz said, "I'm going to organize my photos tomorrow." (plan)

   _____

7. Diego said, "There's a great tutoring center at our school. I'm going to use it in the afternoons." (expect)

   _____

8. Katherine's mother said, "No, you cannot get a tattoo on your leg." (forbid)

   _____

9. The college said, "All students must have a laptop computer." (require)

   _____

10. Yolanda said, "I was majoring in chemistry, but it's too hard. I'm going to change my major." (decide)

    _____

11. Edgar said, "I'm joining the navy when I graduate from high school." (plan)

    _____

12. The teacher said, "You can use your dictionary during the test." (allow)

    _____

4. Choose an adjective from the box. Use the cues and write a sentence about school.

difficult	foolish	helpful	necessary
easy	good	important	stressful
expensive	hard	impossible	unrealistic

1. go to college

   <u>It's expensive to go to college.</u>

2. work and go to school

   _____

3. take notes in class

   _____

4. find time to study

   _____

5. plan a schedule each day

   _____

6. get an A in every course

   _____

7. find a quiet place to study

   _____

8. stay up all night

   _____

9. get enough sleep

   _____

10. make a list of all my assignments

    _____

11. understand chemistry

    _____

12. plan ahead for tests and papers

    _____

5. Listen to six sentences about this picture. Write the three sentences that are true.

shovel
snow
snow blower

1. _____

2. _____

3. _____

6. Listen to the situation. Circle the correct information.

1. a. She forgot to take an umbrella.

   b. She remembered to take an umbrella.

2. a. He knows how to change a flat tire.

   b. He doesn't know how to change a flat tire.

3. a. She hates to iron.

   b. She likes to iron.

4. a. The teacher will allow the students to use their dictionaries on the test.

   b. The teacher won't allow the students to use their dictionaries on the test.

5. a. Tenants are permitted to have pets.

   b. Tenants aren't permitted to have pets.

6. a. He decided to pay the parking fine.

   b. He decided to protest the parking fine.

7. a. She managed to get into the house.

   b. She wasn't able to get into the house.

7. Listen and complete these conversations about each situation.

Conversation 1: Two friends

1. The woman expected her neighbors _to call a tree service_____.

2. Her friend advised her _____.

Conversation 2: Father and son

3. His father didn't allow _____.

4. His father expects _____.

Conversation 3: Two friends

5. Her boss wants _____.

6. Her friend advised _____.

Read about Debra's experience with the grammar test. Then, read the suggestions in the chart, and check the ideas that you think will help you. Then, add two more ideas.

Last week, Debra's teacher announced a grammar test on the past tense. Debra went home and practiced her list of past tense verbs. She looked at the simple form, and wrote the past form. She felt confident that she knew all the past verbs. On the day of the test, the teacher passed out a three-page test. On the first page, the students listened to questions and wrote full sentence answers. On the second page, the students wrote a story about a series of pictures. On the third page, the students looked at a man's schedule and formed questions and answers about his activities. Debra failed the test because she only knew individual words.

It's difficult to study for a test in English. Language is cumulative, so it's not possible to study just one grammar structure or vocabulary list. Some tests, like listening or writing, are almost impossible to study for.

However, it is possible to better prepare yourself for a test. When the teacher announces a test, ask questions to help yourself prepare and study effectively:
- What is the test going to cover?
- How long is the test?
- What kind of questions will be on the test?
- What should we study?
- Can we do a practice test?
- Can we use a dictionary during the test?

Then, begin to study a few days before the test.

		Yes	No
1.	I ask my teacher questions about the test.		
2.	I start to study a few days before the test.		
3.	I study with a partner.		
4.	I review the material in the previous units.		
5.	I study in a quiet place.		
6.	I carefully go over my homework and the exercises in the book.		
7.	Before I begin the exam, I look over the entire test. I check how many points are given for each answer. I spend more time on answers that are worth many points.		
8.	I look over the exam and ask the teacher about any directions I don't understand.		
9.	I try to answer all the questions, especially if they are True/False or multiple choice. If I am not sure of the answer, I make my best guess.		
10.	When I finish, I check the test carefully.		
11.	I edit my writing.		

When I study, I _____.

When I am taking a test, I _____.

Becoming a Citizen

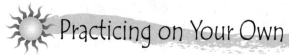 Practicing on Your Own

1. **Match the person in the first column with the action in the second column.**

<u>c</u>	**1.** The mayor is considering	**a.**	building our new deck.
___	**2.** The new citizen anticipates	**b.**	not studying for the test.
___	**3.** The mail carrier can't stand	**c.**	running for re-election.
___	**4.** The plumber recommended	**d.**	painting with bold colors.
___	**5.** The carpenter finished	**e.**	voting in the next election.
___	**6.** The student regrets	**f.**	stealing the man's wallet.
___	**7.** The artist likes	**g.**	working on rainy days.
___	**8.** The musician is practicing	**h.**	installing a new toilet.
___	**9.** The waiter appreciated	**i.**	playing the new song.
___	**10.** The thief admitted	**j.**	receiving a large tip.

2. **Answer these questions. Use a gerund in your answers.**

1. Who do you miss seeing?

   _____

2. What do you enjoy doing on the weekends?

   _____

3. What chore do you dislike doing?

   _____

4. What food do you avoid eating?

   _____

5. How long do you plan on working for your present company?

   _____

6. What movie do you recommend seeing?

   _____

7. Where are you considering moving?

   _____

8. What have you postponed buying?

   _____

9. What do you anticipate doing next year?

   _____

3. Complete these sentences with a gerund. Use the words from the box.

build	pay	receive
get	walk	lose
open	raise	listen

1. Many people are opposed to _____ higher taxes.

2. The schools are overcrowded. I'm in favor of _____ a new school.

3. In this slow economy, he's worried about _____ his job.

4. She's afraid of _____ in the park after dark.

5. I'm tired of _____ to the mayor's promises. I want to see some action.

6. After-school activities prevent teenagers from _____ into trouble.

7. Some people approve of _____ taxes in order to provide medical insurance for everyone.

8. Many senior citizens depend on _____ social security.

9. If he is elected mayor, he plans on _____ a homeless shelter.

4. Combine these sentences with the preposition in parentheses. Use a gerund.

1. Lin filled out the paperwork. Lin waited three years for a visa. (after)

   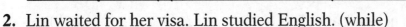
   After filling out the paperwork, Lin waited three years for a visa.

2. Lin waited for her visa. Lin studied English. (while)

   _____

3. Lin arrived in the United States. She spoke English well. (before)

   _____

4. Lin studied English. Lin attended nursing school. (in addition to)

   _____

5. Lin arrived in the United States. She found a job in a hospital. (after)

   _____

6. Lin didn't buy a car. She took the bus to work. (instead of)

   _____

7. Lin lived in the United States for five years. She became a citizen. (after)

   _____

5. (Circle) the correct form—the gerund or the infinitive.

1. I miss   **a.** to see my family.   **(b.)** seeing my family.

2. I appreciate   **a.** to receive a college loan.   **b.** receiving a college loan.

3. It's difficult   **a.** to make close friends.   **b.** making close friends.

4. He resents   **a.** to spend so much on medical care   **b.** spending so much on on medical care.

5. He enjoys   **a.** to drive on good roads.   **b.** driving on good roads.

6. It's possible   **a.** to travel anywhere.   **b.** traveling anywhere.

7. I dislike   **a.** to eat American food.   **b.** eating American food.

8. It's easy   **a.** to go into debt.   **b.** going into debt.

9. My sister advised me   **a.** not to get a credit card   **b.** not getting a credit card.

10. I'm trying   **a.** to find a better job.   **b.** finding a better job.

11. I regret   **a.** not to save more money.   **b.** not saving more money.

12. I'm good at   **a.** to express my opinions.   **b.** expressing my opinions.

6. Complete these sentences about learning English. Some verbs take the gerund form. Some verbs take the infinitive form.

1. I didn't know how _____to speak_____ (speak) English when I arrived in the United States.

2. I have made a lot of progress in _____ (learn) English.

3. At first, I tried _____ (translate) every word.

4. I was nervous about _____ (speak).

5. I was afraid of _____ (make) a mistake.

6. I felt like _____ (cry) when people didn't understand my pronunciation.

7. I practiced _____ (speak) in my bedroom with the door closed.

8. My teacher told us not _____ (memorize) separate words, but to learn new words in a sentence.

9. He encouraged us _____ (talk) to our neighbors and co-workers.

10. He also urged us _____ (read) at least thirty minutes a day.

11. Instead of _____ (stand) close to another speaker, I now stand farther away.

12. It took time to adjust to _____ (call) my teacher by his first name.

13. Here, the teacher expects us _____ (look) him in the eye when we speak.

14. It is impolite _____ (ask) a person about age or income.

15. I will continue _____ (study) this new language.

7. **Restatement.** Ana wrote about her experience coming to the United States. Rewrite each sentence using the verb in parentheses with an infinitive or a gerund.

1. Ana couldn't go to college in her country because her family didn't have enough money. (be able)

   <u>She wasn't able to go to college in her country.</u>

2. They sold their house in order to have enough money to come here. (need)

   _____

3. Her husband came here first. (decide)

   _____

4. He was going to send for her in one year. (expect)

   _____

5. She didn't want to stay behind. (opposed to)

   _____

6. She lived with her brother and sister-in-law, but she wasn't happy there. (upset about)

   _____

7. On her husband's advice, she enrolled in English classes in her country. (urge)

   _____

8. Ana and her husband didn't see one another for three years. (miss)

   _____

9. Right now, she speaks well but her writing is weak. (need/concentrate on)

   _____

10. When her English is stronger, she will study accounting. (plan on)

   _____

8. Listen to each situation or conversation. Complete the sentences. Use a gerund in your answers.

1. He is considering <u>moving back to Portugal</u>.
2. She is interested in _____.
3. They postponed _____.
4. She loves _____.
5. He anticipates _____.
6. He worries about _____.
7. He regrets _____.
8. She complains about _____.
9. He's guilty of _____.
10. She forgot about _____.
11. We are concentrating on _____ before we can buy a house.
12. She is opposed to _____.

9. Listen to two people give their views on different issues in their town. What is the man's view? What is the woman's view? Use the vocabulary from the box to write your sentences.

(be) in favor of	don't agree with
approve of	(be) opposed to
	(be) against

The police department
The man <u>is in favor of hiring more police officers</u>.
The woman <u>is against expanding the department</u>.

Youth center
The man _____.
The woman _____.

Library
The man _____.
The woman _____.

Salary for the mayor
The man _____.
The woman _____.

Reading Charts: The Foreign—Born Population of the United States

These three charts provide information from the 2002 Census. According to the U.S. Census Bureau, *foreign born* means people who were not U.S. citizens at birth.

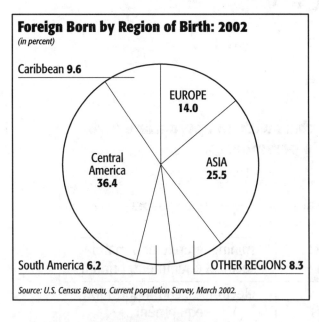

Foreign Born by Region of Birth: 2002
(in percent)

Caribbean **9.6**

EUROPE **14.0**

Central America **36.4**

ASIA **25.5**

South America **6.2**

OTHER REGIONS **8.3**

Source: U.S. Census Bureau, Current population Survey, March 2002.

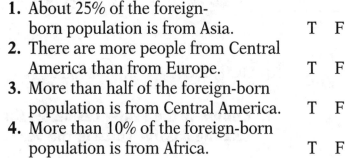

1. About 25% of the foreign-born population is from Asia.   T   F
2. There are more people from Central America than from Europe.   T   F
3. More than half of the foreign-born population is from Central America.   T   F
4. More than 10% of the foreign-born population is from Africa.   T   F

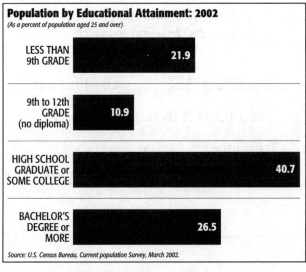

Population by Educational Attainment: 2002
(As a percent of population aged 25 and over)

LESS THAN 9th GRADE	**21.9**
9th to 12th GRADE (no diploma)	**10.9**
HIGH SCHOOL GRADUATE or SOME COLLEGE	**40.7**
BACHELOR'S DEGREE or MORE	**26.5**

Source: U.S. Census Bureau, Current population Survey, March 2002.

5. More than 25% of the foreign born have a college degree.   T   F
6. More than 60% of the foreign born have a high school or college degree.   T   F
7. About 10% of the foreign born have less than a ninth grade education.   T   F

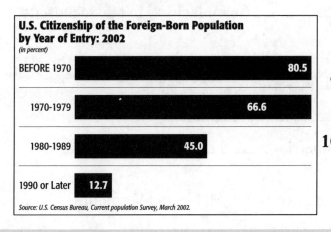

U.S. Citizenship of the Foreign-Born Population by Year of Entry: 2002
(in percent)

BEFORE 1970	**80.5**
1970-1979	**66.6**
1980-1989	**45.0**
1990 or Later	**12.7**

Source: U.S. Census Bureau, Current population Survey, March 2002.

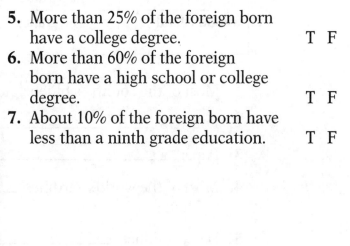

8. More than 60% of the people who entered the United States between 1970 and 1979 have become citizens.   T   F
9. More than half the people who came to the United States after 1980 have become citizens.   T   F
10. The longer a person has lived in the United States, the more likely that person is to become a citizen.   T   F

13 Business and Industry

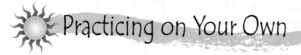

Practicing on Your Own

1. **Complete the sentences below the chart with an appropriate verb. Use the passive voice of the verbs in parentheses.**

State	Agriculture/Fishing	Manufacturing
Maine	blueberries; sardines; lobster	boats; paper
Vermont	dairy products; maple syrup	mining: granite and marble electrical equipment; printing
Massachusetts	cranberries; dairy products	electronics; communication equipment
Rhode Island	grapes	jewelry; electronics; plastic products; medical research

1. Most of the country's blueberries _____**are grown**_____ (grow) in Maine.

2. Lobsters _____ (catch) off the coast of Maine.

3. Paper _____ (produce) in Maine.

4. Most of the world's sardines _____ (catch) in Maine.

5. Dairy products _____ (produce) in Vermont and Massachusetts.

6. Electronics _____ (manufacture) in Massachusetts and Rhode Island.

7. Jewelry _____ (design) and _____ (manufacture) in Rhode Island

8. Boats _____ (build) in Maine.

9. The second largest crop of cranberries _____ (grow) in Massachusetts.

10. Cows _____ (raise) in Maine and Vermont.

2. **Circle** the correct verb forms about different state products.

> Farmers *grow* corn in Iowa.   **active**
> Corn *is grown* in Iowa.   **passive**

1. Paper products   **produce / (are produced)**   in New Hampshire.
2. Clay   **finds / is found**   in the ground of New Hampshire.
3. Engineers   **design / are designed**   jet engines in Connecticut.
4. Maple syrup   **takes / is taken**   from trees in Vermont.
5. Massachusetts   **knows / is known**   for its beaches on Cape Cod.
6. Fishermen   **catch / are caught**   sardines in Maine.
7. Granite and marble   **mine / are mined**   in Vermont.
8. Medical research   **does / is done**   in Rhode Island.
9. Plastic products   **produce / are produced**   in Rhode Island.
10. Many tourists   **visit / are visited**   the beautiful ski areas of Vermont.
11. Lobsters   **trap / are trapped**   for sale in the waters near Maine.
12. Tourists   **enjoy / are enjoyed**   the summer theaters in Massachusetts.

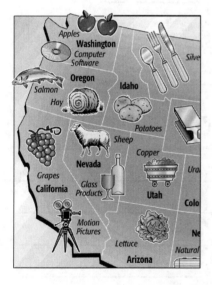

3. **Complete the sentences about the map with the correct verb form of the verbs in the box. Some of the verbs are active; others are passive.**

catch   design   grow   mine   raise   produce

1. Apples _____*are grown*_____ in Washington State.
2. Fishermen _____ salmon off the Pacific Coast of Oregon.
3. Grapes _____ in Northern California.
4. Sheep _____ in Nevada.
5. Farmers _____ potatoes in Idaho.
6. Hay _____ in Oregon.
7. Engineers _____ computer software in Washington State.
8. Copper _____ in Utah.
9. Lettuce _____ in Arizona.
10. Silver _____ in Montana.

4. Look at the product map of Poland and its bordering countries. Write thirteen sentences about the map. Use the verbs from the box and the active or passive form.

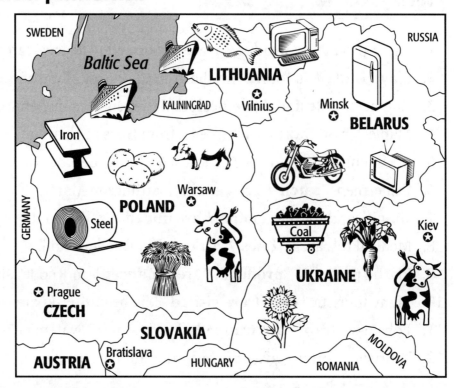

| border | build | catch | design | grow | locate | manufacture | mine | raise | produce |

1. _____
2. _____
3. _____
4. _____
5. _____
6. _____
7. _____
8. _____
9. _____
10. _____
11. _____
12. _____
13. _____

5. How concentrated orange juice is processed. Use the cues to write sentences describing how orange juice is made. Some sentences are passive; others are active. Add extra words where necessary.

1. oranges / ripen / on trees / in orange groves.

   The oranges ripen on trees in orange groves.

2. juice from the oranges / squeeze / and / test

   _____

3. harvesters / pick / oranges / by hand

   _____

4. orange pickers / put / the oranges / into large plastic tubs

   _____

5. oranges / take to processing plant

   _____

6. fruit / wash / and / sort / by size and quality

   _____

7. juice / extract

   _____

8. pulp / and / seeds / remove

   _____

9. water / take out / and / juice / chill

   _____

10. trucks / deliver / juice / to packing plants

   _____

11. filtered water / add / and / juice / pour / into containers

   _____

6. Listen and write the questions. Then, read each question and (circle) the correct answer.

1. _____

   a. Portuguese   **b.** Spanish   **c.** English   **d.** Brazilian

2. _____

   a. Italy   **b.** Poland   **c.** England   **d.** Russia

3. _____

   a. in Arizona   **b.** in New York   **c.** in Texas   **d.** in North Dakota

4. _____

   a. in Colombia   **b.** in South Africa   **c.** in Australia   **d.** in England

5. _____

   a. in Japan   **b.** in China   **c.** in Korea   **d.** in India

6. _____

   a. Morocco   **b.** Italy   **c.** Germany   **d.** Portugal

7. _____

   a. the euro   **b.** the yuan   **c.** the peso   **d.** the yen

8. _____

   a. New York   **b.** Alaska   **c.** California   **d.** Florida

9. _____

   a. every five years   **b.** every four years   **c.** every two years   **d.** every year

10. _____

    a. in Italy   **b.** in Canada   **c.** in India   **d.** in the U.S.

11. _____

    a. every six years   **b.** every five years   **c.** every four years   **d.** every year

12. _____

    a. Bombay, India   **b.** Manila, Phillipines   **c.** Seoul, Korea   **d.** Shanghai, China

13. _____

    a. It's Mother's Day.   **b.** It's Independence Day   **c.** It's Labor Day.

14. _____

    a. in the same country every time   **b.** in a different country every time

Every Monday the weekend's top five movies are announced. The top movie is not always the best movie, but it is the movie that has made the most money. Did you see a movie last weekend? Was it one of the top five movies?

The movie business is a risky business. Many movies are produced every year, but only a few make a great deal of money. Making a movie is often a long and difficult process. First, a writer thinks of an idea for a movie and writes an outline, a brief summary of the movie. If the story is good, a movie studio will buy the rights to the movie. Buying the rights to a movie means that the idea is now owned by the studio. Then, a script, or story with dialogue, is written.

After the script is accepted, the work begins. A movie is made by many small businesses and independent contractors. These smaller companies are needed for every part of the movie-making process. In addition to choosing actors and a director, equipment is rented, special effects are created on computers, costumes are designed, and makeup artists are hired. A crew is hired to operate all of the trucks, cameras, and lights.

The actors for the movie are approved by the studio and selected by the director or a casting director, a person who specializes in selecting actors. Many movies are written for a particular actor such as Harrison Ford, Halle Berry, or Jim Carrey.

After the movie is completed, it is sent to the studio. Sometimes, the movie is shown to test audiences, and parts of the movie are changed to make it more entertaining or interesting for the public. Then, the studio sends the movie to a distribution company. The distribution company shows the movie to people who represent movie theaters. The theater representatives will lease the movie and show it to moviegoers.

Finally, the movie comes to your theater where it will be shown for a specified period of time called an engagement. Can you think of a movie that had a long engagement? How about a movie with a short engagement?

Read and put the steps of the movie-making process in order from 1 to 10.

_____ **a.** Actors are chosen.

_____ **b.** The script is accepted by a studio.

_____ **c.** The movie is leased by a distributor.

_____ **d.** The movie is shown at theaters.

_____ **e.** The script is written.

_____ **f.** The movie is leased for an engagement.

_____ **g.** The actors are approved by the studio.

__1__ **h.** A writer has an idea and writes an outline of a movie.

_____ **i.** Equipment is rented and a crew is hired.

_____ **j.** The movie's rights are purchased by a studio.

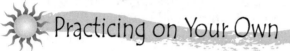

14 Technology Today

Practicing on Your Own

1. **Medical technology.** Match each invention and its use.

_____ 1. A thermometer   **a.** allows a doctor to listen to a patient's lungs and heart.

_____ 2. A stethoscope   **b.** is a radioactive element that can kill cancer cells.

_____ 3. An electrocardiograph   **c.** measures a patient's temperature.

_____ 4. Anesthesia   **d.** is a picture of bones and other internal body parts.

_____ 5. An X-ray   **e.** puts a patient to sleep and reduces pain during an operation.

_____ 6. Radium   **f.** shows a patient's heart activity.

2. **Inventions in medicine.** Complete with the passive voice. Some sentences are in the present tense and some are in the past tense.

1. The thermometer __was invented__ (invent) by Santorio Santorio in 1612.
2. Before the thermometer, a patient's temperature _____ (determine) by feeling the forehead.
3. Today, electronic thermometers _____ (use) in many hospitals.
4. The first stethoscope _____ (make) of wood.
5. A stethoscope _____ the most widely _____ (use) medical instrument today.
6. Before 1850, operations _____ (perform) without anesthesia.
7. At first, ether _____ (use) to put people to sleep and reduce pain.
8. Soon, other anesthetics _____ (develop) that were not as dangerous as ether.
9. X-ray technology _____ (develop) by Wilhelm Roentgen.
10. With X-rays, doctors can see exactly where a bone _____ (break).
11. Radium _____ (discover) by Marie Curie in 1898.
12. Radium _____ (use) to kill cancer cells.
13. The electrocardiograph _____ (invent) by William Einthoven.
14. With the electrocardiograph, a graph _____ (make) of a patient's heartbeat.

3. Camera technology. Change these sentences from active to passive voice.

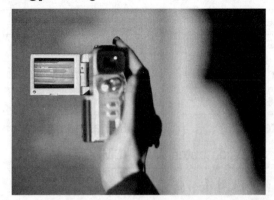

1. Before 1888, photographers used separate plates for each photograph.
   <u>Before 1888, separate plates were used for each photograph.</u>

2. Kodak introduced the first commercial camera in 1888.

   _____

3. Kodak manufactured the first easy-to-use camera in 1900.

   _____

4. The first year, Kodak sold 150,000 cameras.

   _____

5. Paul Vierkotter invented the flash bulb.

   _____

6. Inventors developed color film in 1935.

   _____

7. Edwin Land invented the instant picture camera.

   _____

8. He first sold the cameras in Boston.

   _____

9. Fuji introduced the disposable camera.

   _____

10. Both NASA[1] and private industry developed digital imagery photography.

    _____

11. Companies introduced digital cameras in 1994.

    _____

[1] National Aeronautics and Space Administration

4. Communication technology. Complete these questions in the passive voice.

1832	Telegraph	Samuel Morse
1876	Telephone	Alexander G. Bell
1895	Radio	Guglielmo Marconi
1927	Television	Philo Farnsworth
1957	Satellites	Soviet Union
1981	Personal computer	IBM

1. By whom <u>was the telegraph invented</u> _____?

   It was invented by Samuel Morse.

2. How _____?

   Messages were transmitted by a series of dots and dashes.

3. When _____?

   It was invented in 1876.

4. Where _____?

   The telephone was first demonstrated at an exhibition in Philadelphia.

5. By whom _____?

   It was invented by Guglielmo Marconi.

6. When _____?

   The first radio station was created in 1920.

7. By whom _____?

   The first complete TV system was developed by Philo Farnsworth.

8. Where _____?

   The first TV show was broadcast from the New York World's Fair in 1939.

9. What _____?

   The first satellite was named Sputnik.

10. When _____?

    The first weather satellite was launched in 1960.

11. When _____?

    The personal computer was introduced in 1981.

5. Household inventions. Complete the sentences about these common household inventions in the active or passive voice.

1917	Sneakers	Charles Goodyear
1948	Velcro	George de Mestral
1946	Teflon cookware	Roy Plunkett (DuPont)
1947	Microwave oven	Perry Spencer (Raytheon)
1976	Pop-top can	Ermal Fraze
1969	Smoke alarm	Randolph Smith and Kenneth House
1971	VCR	Charles Ginsbury and team
1973	Plastic soda bottle	Nathaniel Wyeth
1995	DVD technology	Many companies

1. Charles Goodyear _____made_____ (make) the first sneakers in 1917.

2. Velcro _____ (invent) by George de Mestral. It _____ (use) to fasten two materials together. Many companies _____ (use) Velcro on their clothing products.

3. Roy Plunkett _____ (invent) Teflon in 1946. Teflon _____ (apply) to cookware eight years later. Many cooks now _____ (use) non-stick pots and pans.

4. The microwave oven _____ (invent) by Perry Spencer in 1947. The first microwave ovens _____ (weigh) 750 pounds and _____ (cost) $5,000.

5. Randolph Smith and Kenneth House _____ (develop) the first battery-operated smoke detectors for homes. Today, smoke detectors _____ (require) in homes, schools, and apartment buildings.

6. VCRs _____ (introduce) in 1971. They _____ _____ (allow) families to rent movies at video stores. In 1995, many companies _____ (work) together to develop DVD technology. Today, more DVD machines _____ (sell) than VCR players.

7. The pop-top can _____ (develop) by Ermal Fraze. The top _____ (stay) attached and _____ (negative—cause) litter. Before 1973, soda _____ (bottle) in glass bottles. Then, Nathaniel Wyeth _____ (develop) a plastic bottle that could hold carbonated beverages.

6. Write each question you hear next to the correct answer.

1. _____   A few hours later.

2. _____ $10,000.

3. _____   Like an old woman.

4. _Which bank was robbed?_____   The First National Bank.

5. _____   In a park near the bank.

6. _____   No, no one was injured.

7. _____   At 10 A.M.

7. Listen to this report of a snowstorm in Cleveland, Ohio. How was the city affected?

1. _All schools and colleges were closed._____

2. _____

3. _____

4. _____

5. _____

6. _____

8. Listen to this report of a forest fire. Then, answer the questions.

1. How many acres has the fire destroyed?

   _____

2. How many residents live in Stanton?

   _____

3. How long were they given to evacuate?

   _____

4. How many homes were destroyed? _____

5. How were the three fire fighters injured? _____

6. What is the weather forecast? _____

For almost 100 years, inventors experimented with the technology behind photography. The first cameras were large, heavy, and difficult to use. Only professional photographers were able to use the technology.

George Eastman was interested in developing an easy-to-use, affordable camera. The first Kodak camera was introduced in 1888. It cost $25, an expensive item at the time. The camera was preloaded with film for 100 pictures. When the camera was full, the owner mailed the entire camera back to Kodak. The film was removed and processed; then, a new roll of film was loaded into the camera. Kodak mailed the pictures and the camera back to the owner.

Eastman continued to develop camera technology and in 1900 introduced "the Brownie," the first camera for common use. This camera, which only cost a dollar, held a roll of film with six exposures. In just eight years, over eight million of these cameras were sold and photography became a popular hobby.

Advances in camera and film technology developed quickly. Cameras with 35-mm film were introduced in 1924. At first, only black and white film was available. Modern color film was developed in 1935.

Until 1948, all film was returned to the manufacturer for processing or it was developed by amateur photographers in their darkrooms. In 1947, Edwin Land developed a new system of taking and processing film. All of the chemicals necessary to develop a picture were attached to the photosensitive paper. One minute after taking a photo, the paper was peeled off the photo and the image was available. Polaroid-Land cameras were first sold in Boston in 1948. At first, the cameras could only take black and white pictures, but by 1963, instant color pictures were available.

Disposable cameras were first introduced by Fuji in 1986. The company prefers the name "single-use cameras" because it is committed to recycling most parts of the camera.

The technology for digital imagery was developed by both NASA and private industry. In 1994, the first digital cameras for consumers were introduced. At first, the cameras were expensive and the quality of the pictures was not as clear as regular cameras. Over the past ten years, prices have dropped and the cameras are easier to use. In 2003, more digital cameras were sold than film cameras.

Complete this chart with five more developments in camera technology.

Date	Inventor	Invention
1888	George Eastman	First commercial camera

15 Country Music

Practicing on Your Own

Shakira

Faith Hill

Mariah Carey

1. **Complete the sentences about each singer. Use *who, whose,* or *which*.**

   1. The singer _____ photograph is in the middle sings country music.
   2. Faith Hill, _____ is married to the country singer, Tim McGraw, sold 472,000 copies of her album, "Cry," the first week it was released.
   3. Faith Hill, _____ album, "Breathe" has sold more than ten million copies, performs many concerts every year.
   4. Shakira was born in Barrangquilla, _____ is located on the coast of Colombia.
   5. Shakira, _____ name means "woman full of grace," is the youngest of eight children.
   6. Shakira was lucky to have some help from Gloria Estefan, _____ became her manager and producer.
   7. For three years, Shakira starred in a television soap opera, _____ was produced in Colombia.
   8. Maria Carey was married to a man _____ record company produced her first album.
   9. Carey's first album, _____ was named "Mariah Carey," had four hit songs.
   10. Mariah Carey, _____ became a star in 1990, has sold over eighty million albums.

2. **Match each phrase in Group A with the correct adjective clause from Group B.**

A

__b__ 1. Celine Dion is a popular singer,

____ 2. Celine Dion married her manager,

____ 3. Celine Dion sang the theme for the movie "Titanic,"

____ 4. Dion has recorded songs in French,

____ 5. Dion and her husband have a child,

____ 6. Dion performed in a Las Vegas hotel,

B

a. which is one of the native languages of Quebec, the province where she is from.

b. whose record sales have made her a superstar.

c. who has directed her career for many years.

d. which gave her a three-year contract.

e. which won eleven Oscar nominations, including "Best Picture."

f. whom they named René Charles.

3. **Read the sentences. The adjective clauses are in the wrong position. Circle the adjective clause and draw an arrow to the correct position in the sentence.**

1. Enrique Iglesias, was born in Spain, who became a pop star in 1995.

2. Iglesias has been influenced by many rock singers, whose father is also a famous singer.

3. The woman was walking her dog, who was talking on her cell phone.

4. When she played the role of Selena, Jennifer Lopez's big career move happened in 1997.

5. Hip hop music, which includes clothes, jewelry, and language, is influenced by urban culture.

6. Mrs. Stanford made a delicious cake for her daughter, which was covered with chocolate.

7. Celia Cruz, died of cancer in 2003, whom fans called the "Queen of Salsa."

8. Cruz was honored, where a street was renamed after her, in Miami.

4. When clauses. Complete the adjective clauses.

> I'll never forget the day when I saw Elton John live in concert.
> 1982 was the year when my first son was born.

1. June is the month when _____.

2. _____ was the year when _____.

3. Thanksgiving is a time when _____.

4. Weekends are the time when _____.

5. _____ was the month when _____.

6. _____ is the date when _____.

7. Saturday night is the night when _____.

8. I'll never forget the day when _____.

5. Where clauses. Combine the sentences. Use the second sentence as an adjective clause with *where*.

1. The building is very old. He lives in that building.

   The building where he lives is very old. _____

2. That is the concert hall. My cousin performed there.

   _____

3. This is the music store. I can find music from my county here.

   _____

4. That room is the Academic Learning Center. Students can practice English in that room.

   _____

5. That is the building. I study English in that building.

   _____

6. Last weekend I went to a park. I heard a beautiful concert in that park.

   _____

6. Rewrite the following paragraph. Use adjective clauses.

Justin Timberlake was born on January 31,1981, in Memphis, Tennessee. He is known for his relationship with the boy band, N'Sync. N'Sync enjoyed enormous popularity in the late 90s. N'Sync had a number of bestselling singles and albums. Timberlake had a very public relationship with Britney Spears. Timberlake was one of N'Sync's most popular members. Britney Spears's career was also doing well. In 2002, Timberlake started his solo career. In that same year, Timberlake and Spears broke up. Timberlake worked on his first solo album. He was assisted by Brian McKnight and Mario Winans. Brian McKnight and Mario Winans had good reputations in R&B music. Timberlake also worked on the album with other superstars. Those superstars included Janet Jackson.

Justin Timberlake, who is known for his relationship with the boy band, N'Sync, was born on January 31, 1981, in Memphis, Tennessee.

7. Listen and fill in the adjective clauses.

1. Bono is the lead singer for U-2, _____
   _____

2. Bono was born in Ireland, _____
   _____

3. Bono and a group of other high-school students formed
   a band, _____

4. Bono tries to write songs _____

5. Bono likes to talk about music with his fans, _____
   _____

8. Listen and take notes in the space below about Bono and U-2.

> ```
> 
> 
> 
> 
> 
> 
> 
> ```

9. Use your notes and write answers to the questions.

1. When did Bono begin playing the guitar?
   _____

2. What subjects did he enjoy in high school?
   _____

3. Why was Bono chosen as lead singer?
   _____

4. What kinds of music have influenced Bono?
   _____

5. What does he want to do during a live performance?
   _____

6. With whom has he discussed world issues?
   _____

7. What causes is Bono interested in?
   _____

bluegrass music—a form of country music that features banjo, string or electric bass, and dobro guitar—named after Kentucky, The Bluegrass State.

When you hear the names Arzamastev, Olkhovsky, Borzilova, Ostrovsky, Salnikova, and Toshinsky, you probably do not think of country music. Those names are the members of a country music band named Bering Strait. All members grew up in Obninsk, Russia, but have found a new home in the United States where they have been performing country music.

How did the six band members end up playing country music? It all started with music lessons in Russia and a guitar teacher, who was a fan of bluegrass music. The teacher introduced Ilya Toshinsky, his student, to the banjo, and Ilya quickly became comfortable playing the new instrument. Then, the teacher decided to form a bluegrass band. All the band members had strong musical training.

As Russia began changing, American culture, including music, grew in popularity. The band performed on Russian TV, recorded songs for English lessons, and built a reputation.

Everything changed in 1992, when Ilya at the age of fourteen, attended the Tennessee Banjo Institute. Ilya had such a good experience and learned so much that he knew he would return. A year later the entire band was in Oak Ridge, Tennessee, the sister city of Obninsk. The band was still playing bluegrass music, but they were becoming more interested in playing country music.

After the band decided to concentrate on country music, they knew that they had to move to the United States where they would be able to learn from the best. At first, they were alone. Later, they found a manager, Mike Kinnamon, who helped them with their careers. Kinnamon even let them live in his home while the band was trying to find a record deal.

In 1999, the band signed its first recording contract, but due to many changes at the company, they was not able to record. After a few years of bad luck and no contract, the group was thinking about returning to Russia. In 2002, almost three years later, the band finally recorded a debut album, Bering Strait. In 2003, Bering Strait was nominated for a prestigious Grammy award for Best Country Instrumental Performance. It was the first nomination for a Russian band.

Read the passage. <u>Underline</u> and number the answers to these questions.

1. Why is this band unusual?
2. How did the band get started?
3. Why was the Tennessee Banjo Institute important to the band's career?
4. Why did the band members move to the United States?
5. Who helped them while they were waiting for a contract?
6. How do you know that the band found success?

Audio Script

Unit 1: Education

Page 6

7. Listen and circle *Now* or *Every day.*
1. I'm eating lunch. **2.** I go to school from 9:00 to 12:00.
3. We eat dinner at 7:00. **4.** We're watching television.
5. They work at a department store. **6.** The students are taking a test. **7.** They're listening to conversations in the learning center. **8.** The students study in the library.

Page 6

8. Listen and write a short answer.
1. Is there a map in your classroom? **2.** Are the students taking a test? **3.** Does your class meet on Saturdays?
4. Is English easy? **5.** Is there a student from China in your class? **6.** Are the students in your class usually on time? **7.** Does your class meet in the evenings? **8.** Is it time for your class?

Page 6

9. Listen to the description of Miami-Dade Community College. Take notes.

Miami-Dade Community College is a public, two-year community college. It has six campuses located in southeastern Florida. Miami-Dade was founded in 1960 and is one of the largest community colleges in the United States. It has an annual enrollment of approximately 55,000 students including 2,500 international students. The college employs 3,388 faculty. In 2003, full-time tuition cost $1,583 for Florida residents.

Miami-Dade offers an education to anyone who wants one. Anyone can enroll at the college. The college offers an associate in arts degree and an associate in science degree. It also offers certificate programs.

Students can participate in many activities sponsored by more than 100 organizations. There are student newspapers, social clubs, and musical groups for the students. Because more than half of the student population is Spanish-speaking, there are also theater groups that perform in English and Spanish.

Students who live far away or out of state must find places to live in the Miami area. There are no dormitories for the students.

Unit 2: Colonial Times (1607–1776)

Page 12

6. Compare life today with life fifty years ago. Write each sentence you hear next to the correct answer.
Police used to match fingerprints. People used to type reports. People used to watch black and white TV.
A movie ticket used to cost twenty-five cents. People used to wear glasses.

Page 12

7. The box below includes the names of several presidents. Read the statements under the box. Then, listen and write the name of the correct president.

Have you ever seen a movie starring Ronald Reagan? Before he became active in politics, President Reagan acted in several films. He played different roles, including soldier, football player, and cowboy.

President Franklin D. Roosevelt was elected to office four times. He died in office in 1945. After his presidency, the Congress passed a law that presidents could only serve two terms, that is, eight years.

George Washington did not live in the White House. During his presidency, the White House was under construction. The second president, John Adams, moved into the White House in 1800.

While Bill Clinton was president, his wife, Hillary Rodham Clinton, ran for political office. She was elected as senator from New York State in November, 2000, while her husband was still in office.

While Richard Nixon was serving his second term in office, there was a political scandal. Nixon resigned as president in August, 1974. The vice president became the president.

George W. Bush's father, George H.W. Bush was the forty first president of the United States. John Quincy Adams was the sixth president. His father, John Adams, was the second president of the United States.

Page 12

8. Listen and write each question you hear next to the correct answer.
What country are you from? When did you come to the United States? Did you come alone? How old were you? Who did you live with? Was it easy to find a job? Could you speak English?

Unit 3: Family Matters

Page 18

6. Before getting married, couples should discuss many important issues. Listen and write the questions.
1. Where will we live? **2.** Why are we getting married?
3. How many children do we want? **4.** Who is going to take care of the children? **5.** Are we both going to work?
6. How are we going to make decisions? **7.** How are we going to handle our finances? **8.** How are we going to divide the household chores? **9.** Where will we spend our vacations?

Page 18

7. Listen to these short conversations. Then, complete the sentences.
1. Woman: Mom, I have to work overtime from 5:00 to 6:00 today. Can you watch the kids? **Mom:** Sure, Susan. I'll come over and watch them. **2. Man:** What time are the visiting hours? **Woman:** They're from 2:00 to 5:00. **Man:** Let's stop at the florist and pick up some flowers for your sister. **Woman:** Good idea. **3. Mom:** Did you clean your room yet? **Son:** Not yet. Just let me watch the rest of the movie. **Mom:** OK. **4. Girl 1:** Can you go to the mall this afternoon? **Girl 2:** Yes, but not until about 3:00. I'm studying for my biology test. **5. Man 1:** Where are you going on vacation? **Man 2:** To the beach. **Man 1:** What are you going to do? **Man 2:** Fish. I'm going to fish every day. **6. Man:** Did you register for college yet? **Woman:** No, I didn't take the entrance exam yet. **7. Woman:** When are we going to leave? **Man:** At 10:00. **Woman:** Did you put gas in the car? **Man:** I'm on my way now. **8. Woman:** You're 30 minutes late for work. **Man:** I was stuck in traffic. There was a big accident. **Woman:** Do you have a cell phone? **Man:** Yes. **Woman:** Next time, call and let us know.

Page 18

8. Listen and write the short answers. Use your imagination!
1. Is he proposing to her? **2.** Does he love her? **3.** Is she going to say "Yes"? **4.** Did he buy her a beautiful diamond? **5.** Is she surprised? **6.** Is this his first marriage? **7.** Are they going to get married this summer? **8.** Did she expect this proposal? **9.** Is she going to call her parents tonight? **10.** Will they live happily ever after?

Unit 4: Comparisons—Global and Local

Page 24

9. Three botanical gardens. Listen and complete.
1. The University of Padova has one of the oldest botanical gardens in the world. **2.** Padova is the home of one of the earliest medical schools. **3.** The Butchart Gardens aren't as old as Padova's, but they attract many more visitors. **4.** The most popular time to visit the Butchart Gardens is during the summer. **5.** Brooklyn Botanic Garden has one of the finest rose gardens in the United States. **6.** Brooklyn Botanic Garden has one of the most beautiful collections of Japanese cherry trees outside of Japan.

Page 24

10. Listen and complete the chart.

The Butchart Gardens are located in Victoria, British Columbia in Canada. The gardens were founded in 1904 by a wealthy husband and wife. There are 55 acres for the public to enjoy. Adults pay $20 for admission and children pay only $1.50. In the summer, the gardens are open at 9 A.M. and close at 10:30 P.M. One of the special features in the spring is the garden of over 100,000 tulips.

The Brooklyn Botanic Garden is located in Brooklyn, New York. It was founded in 1910 by New York State on 52 acres of land. Admission for adults is $5.00, but all children are free. In the summer, the garden is open from 8 A.M. to 6 P.M. from Tuesday to Friday. On weekends, the garden is open from 10 A.M. to 6 P.M. The garden is closed on Mondays. One of the gardens special features is its more than 200 cherry trees, which is one of the best collections outside of Japan.

The University of Padova's Botanic Garden is located in Padova, Italy. The garden was founded in 1545 at the home of one of the earliest medical schools in the world. The garden is on 4.94 acres of land. Admission for adults is $4.35 and $1.35 for children. In the summer, the garden is open from 9 A.M. to 6 P.M. It closes for lunch from 1 P.M. to 3 P.M. The garden's specialty is its collection of approximately 6,000 medicinal plants that the University grows for medical study and exhibition.

Page 24

11. Listen and write complete answers to the questions.
1. Which garden was founded the earliest? **2.** Which garden is the largest? **3.** Which garden is older than the Butchart Gardens? **4.** Which garden charges the most for adults? **5.** Which garden charges the least for children? **6.** Which garden has the longest summer hours?

Unit 5: Leisure Activities

Page 30

9. Listen and write the correct tag.
1. You're a student,... **2.** The test was difficult,... **3.** They arrived late,... **4.** He likes to paint, ... **5.** You play volleyball,... **6.** You have a passport,... **7.** She doesn't like to fish,... **8.** It isn't valuable,... **9.** He wasn't a cook,... **10.** They weren't in the office, ...

Page 30

10. Listen and number the correct answers from 1 to 10.
1. How much did your used car cost? **2.** How long is this play? **3.** How often do you run in the park? **4.** How far is it from your home to downtown? **5.** How many books did you buy? **6.** How do you get to work? **7.** How many hours a week does your class meet? **8.** How many days will you stay in the city? **9.** How was the movie? **10.** How often does he have to take this medicine?

Page 30

11. Listen to each conversation and answer the questions.
Conversation 1
Ben: So, here you are again, Emma.
Emma: Yes, I love spending time here.
Ben: What are you doing?
Emma: I'm pulling out weeds and I'm moving about ten plants.
Ben: That sounds like a big job.
Emma: It is, but I'm enjoying it. It's a beautiful day, isn't it?
Ben: Yes, it is. I'd like to help you, but my allergies are acting up.
Emma: Alright. See you later, Ben
Conversation 2
Woman: That's very nice.
Man: Thank you, but it's really not so good. The colors are all wrong.

Woman: No, the colors are just right.
Man: This is my first painting class. I took drawing last semester.
Woman: Really? This is only your first class? I can't believe it. This is my second semester, and my paintings still look terrible.
Man: Which one is yours?
Woman: That one over there.
Man: Oh, that one. It's interesting. I especially like the bananas.
Woman: Uh, those aren't bananas. Those are apples.
Man: Oh, excuse me.

Unit 6: Driving

Page 36

8. Listen to people talk about driving. Complete with *can* or *can't*.
1. I **can drive** a manual transmission. **2.** He **can't drive** in the city. **3.** Vehicles **can't pass** on the right. **4.** I **can handle** a large vehicle. **5.** She **can park** an SUV. **6.** The children **can watch** videos in the back seat. **7.** We **can't drive** over 25 miles per hour in this area. **8.** She **can get** her license in two months. **9.** He **can't borrow** the car without his parents' permission. **10.** They **can't ride** in a car without car seats.

Page 36

9. Listen and complete the sentences about Leo's new job. Use *must* or *must not* and an appropriate verb.
Boss: Welcome to Action Industries.
Leo: Thank you. I'm excited about working here.
Boss: Good. Let me tell you a few of our rules. First of all, don't wear your uniform outside the company. Change into your uniform in the employee locker room.
Leo: Change here. Got it.
Boss: Always wear your name tag. Security is important.
Leo: Wear my name tag. Right.
Boss: When you're ready to enter the work area, punch the time clock. Work starts exactly at 8:30.
Leo: At 8:30. Okay.
Boss: Do not take personal phone calls during company time unless there's an emergency. There are two breaks during the day and thirty minutes for lunch. You can make calls then.
Leo: No calls during company time and thirty minutes for lunch. That's better than I used to have at my old job. We only had fifteen minutes.
Boss: There's required overtime every fall. That's our busy season.
Leo: How often do I have to work overtime?
Boss: Once a week. If you work more, the company will pay you double time.
Leo: Double time? Good.
Boss: That's it. Please go to Human Resources and complete your paperwork. I'll see you tomorrow morning.
Leo: At 8:30.

Page 36

10. Listen and write a suggestion for each person. Use *should* or *shouldn't*.
1. **Male:** My apartment is a mess, and my parents are coming for a visit. **2. Male:** I don't know what's wrong with my car. I just had it at the mechanic last week. **3. Female:** I'd like to take another language class. I've already studied Italian. I'm not sure what to take next. **4. Female:** I'm really enjoying my English class, but I need more conversation practice. **5. Male:** I'm exhausted. Working overtime every weekend and almost every day doesn't give me enough time for my family. **6. Female:** I feel terrible. I went to the doctor, but I still feel miserable.

Unit 7: Sports

Page 42

6. Listen to these statements about sports. Is the action continuing or is the action finished?
1. He played baseball. **2.** They've been hiking in the mountains. **3.** They've been skiing. **4.** She ran in the park. **5.** They watched a tennis match. **6.** She's been swimming. **7.** My favorite team won the championship. **8.** He's been fishing in the ocean. **9.** He's been lifting weights at the gym. **10.** We saw a great soccer game. **11.** She's been

coaching the team for a long time. **12.** I've been going to the gym five times a week.

Page 42

7. Listen to these short conversations. Circle the true information.
Conversation 1
A: How's the team doing?
B: At the beginning of the season, we were losing most of our games. The players are beginning to feel more confident. We've won our last five games.
Conversation 2
A: You look great.
B: Thanks. I've been going to the gym almost every day.
A: Are you on a diet?
B: No, I'm not. But all this exercise is really helping.
Conversation 3
A: How's Larry after his knee operation? Is he running again?
B: He was feeling better, but then he tried to start running and now his knee is hurting him again. The doctor told him to wait two more months before running again.
Conversation 4
A: Are you still using the gym every day?
B: When I first joined, I used the gym four or five times a week. I only go about once a week now.
Conversation 5
A: How's school this semester?
B: Much better! Last semester was really difficult. But now, I have good grades in all my classes.
Conversation 6
A: How's David?
B: I'm not going out with him anymore.
A: You went out for two years!
B: I know, but I'm seeing someone new now.

Page 42

8. Listen to the information about Stan and look at the time line. Then, answer each question in a complete sentence.
Stan's first job was in New York City. He was a taxi driver for the Yellow Cab Taxi Company. He liked the passengers, but the traffic was terrible. He worked in New York from 1990 to 1995. Then, he moved to San Francisco. Because Stan had a lot of experience driving, he was able to get a job as a bus driver. He drove up and down the hills of San Francisco from 1995 to 2000. Then, Stan moved to Boston where he found a good job at a transcontinental trucking company. He drives furniture, toys, electronic equipment, and other manufactured items from Boston to other cities all over the United States. He likes his job a lot.
1. What did Stan do in New York? **2.** How many years did he drive a bus? **3.** How long has Stan been driving a truck? **4.** When did he leave New York? **5.** How long did Stan live in San Francisco? **6.** Where does he live now? **7.** How long has Stan been living in Boston?

Unit 8: Changes

Page 47

6. There is a hurricane warning in Florida. Listen to these ten sentences about the picture. Write the six sentences that are true.
The tree has fallen down.
The wind has begun to blow.
They have been preparing for the hurricane.
They have put their cars in the garage already.
It has begun to rain.
They have evacuated.
They've put their yard furniture in the garage.
They have just closed the garage door.
The woman has just returned from the store.
She has bought extra food and water.

Page 48

7. Listen to the questions. Write the answers in the correct tense—present perfect or past.
1. Have you received your paycheck yet? **2.** Have you seen the new movie? **3.** Has the plane arrived yet? **4.** Have you taken your vacation yet? **5.** Have you registered to vote? **6.** Has he found his wallet? **7.** Have you fixed the light yet? **8.** Have you called the doctor? **9.** Has she had the baby yet? **10.** Has the bank closed yet? **11.** Have you

eaten at the new Mexican restaurant yet? **12.** Have you spoken to the boss yet?

Page 48

8. Luisa is expecting a baby is three weeks. Listen to the preparations for the new baby. Check *Completed* or *Not completed*. Then, write seven sentences about the information in the chart using *already* or *yet*.
Luisa is pregnant with her first child. She's due in three weeks. She and her husband Alberto have taken care of many of the preparations for the baby, but they still have several things to do.
Luisa doesn't know if she's going to have a boy or a girl. She and her husband have already chosen a boy's name. They both like the name Michael, but they haven't chosen a girl's name yet.
The baby's room is almost ready. They've painted the room yellow, but they haven't ordered any baby furniture yet. Luisa has already bought a car seat, too, because the hospital requires that all babies go home in car seats.
Luisa and Alberto have taken child birth classes already because Alberto is going to stay with Luisa in the delivery room. Alberto has just bought a new digital camera to take pictures of the new baby.
Luisa hasn't stopped working yet. She has an office job, so she can sit down most of the day. She's going to stop working next week. Luisa has already packed her suitcase to take to the hospital in case the baby comes early.

Unit 9: Job Performance

Page 54

6. Listen to these sentences about work. Is the action or job finished? Circle *Finished* or *Not finished*.
1. I sent the packages. **2.** I've typed two reports so far. **3.** I delivered twelve orders. **4.** He's baked 50 cakes, so he's taking a break. **5.** I called Mr. Sanders at 10 o'clock. **6.** She fixed the copy machine this morning. **7.** He's seen five patients since he came in this morning. **8.** He installed the new air-conditioning system. It took him two days. **9.** They've taken 36 photographs already, so they're putting a new roll of film in the camera. **10.** He's cleaned ten rooms and he has ten more to go.

Page 54

7. Listen to each sentence. Then, circle the sentence with the same meaning.
1. Roberto worked for Ace Electronics from 2000 to 2003. He works at a different company now. **2.** Sylvia began to deliver packages at 8:00 A.M. There are ten more packages on the truck. **3.** Susan taught first grade for ten years. Then, she taught second grade for ten years. Susan is now teaching third grade. **4.** Kenia is a college student. Her first major was science, but she didn't like all the laboratory work. She changed her major to accounting, but now she thinks it's boring. She's trying to decide what to major in. **5.** Cesar is a photographer. He's developing the pictures he took at a client's wedding last weekend. **6.** Joe is a baseball manager. His team is having a great season. **7.** Laura is a loan officer at a bank. Before she went home, she approved twenty loans and she rejected five loans. **8.** Because of the snow storm, Tony had to close his barber shop early.

Page 54

8. Look at the time line and listen to Amy's job history. Answer each question in a complete sentence.
1. How many times has Amy changed jobs? **2.** When did she sell appliances? **3.** Has she ever sold furniture? **4.** What does Amy sell now? **5.** When did Amy start at Samson Insurance? **6.** How long has she been selling insurance? **7.** How long has Amy been in sales?

Unit 10: Regrets and Possibilities

Page 60

7. Listen and complete the sentences.
1. You should've put on your coat. **2.** I shouldn't have turned on my phone. **3.** He couldn't have taken that flight. **4.** They might have missed the bus. **5.** She could have taken a taxi. **6.** It may not have been on time. **7.** She must not have heard the phone. **8.** They must have left

it at home on the table. **9.** He might not have seen the sign for the exit. **10.** She may have decided not to come with us.

8. Listen and circle the correct answers.
1. M: I should've taken a different job. **2. M:** I should've moved to a colder climate. **3. F:** I shouldn't have bought such a large car. **4. M:** I should've mailed the checks earlier. **5. F:** I shouldn't have left home so early. **6. M:** I shouldn't have parked my car there. **7. F:** I should've listened to my brother. **8. F:** I should've looked here sooner. I wasted so much time. **9. M:** I shouldn't have eaten the last piece. **10. F:** I should've written down the directions.

Unit 11: Let's Get Organized
Page 66
5. Listen to six sentences about this picture. Write the three sentences that are true.
1. This man likes to shovel snow. **2.** This man hates to shovel snow. **3.** He wants to move to a warmer climate. **4.** It's easy to shovel snow. **5.** His son volunteered to help him. **6.** He needs to buy a snow blower.

Page 66
6. Listen to the situation. Circle the correct information.
1. I'm all wet! I have to listen to the weather forecast in the morning. **2.** I really like to ride my bike. But, what am I supposed to do if I'm five or ten miles from my house and I get a flat tire? **3.** I threw away my iron. If I look at the tag on a blouse and it's got that little symbol for an iron, you know, to show that you have to iron it, I just put it back on the clothes rack. **4.** Students, for your reading test tomorrow, don't bring your dictionaries to class. You need to figure out any new words from the story. **5.** Did you see this notice we got from the landlord? He heard a dog barking last time he was in the building. He's really upset. **6.** I got a ticket for parking overtime at a meter yesterday. But the meter was broken. I'm going to go to court and explain this to the judge. **7.** I locked myself out of the house yesterday. I went around back and saw that the bathroom window was open. My son climbed in the window and opened the door.

Page 66
7. Listen and complete these conversations about each situation.
Conversation 1: Two friends
Eva: Our neighbor's tree fell into our yard in that bad storm last week. And that tree is still in our backyard.
Frank: Is it just a small tree?
Eva: Small tree? It's a huge tree, about eighty feet tall. The kids can't play in the backyard anymore.
Frank: Have you spoken to them?
Eva: Yes, we spoke to them and asked them to call a tree service, but they haven't done anything.
Frank: It's time to call a lawyer.
Conversation 2: Father and son
Son: Dad, I'm going over Steve's.
Father: Don't you have a science test tomorrow?
Son: Yeah, but I know the material. It's easy.
Father: You failed your last science test. Call Steve and tell him you can't see him tonight. You need to study.
Conversation 3: Two friends
W: My boss keeps asking me to work more hours. I told her I was going to college and that I could only work on weekends. But she keeps assigning me hours during the week.
M: Talk to her again. She isn't being fair to you.

Unit 12: Citizenship
Page 72
8. Listen to each situation or conversation. Complete the sentences. Use a gerund in your answers.

1. M: My two brothers and my sister still live in Portugal. I might go back there some day. **2. M:** Are you going to become a citizen? **F:** I think so. I need to find out more about the application process. **3. M:** We were going to take a vacation to Alaska. But then my mother got sick. We're hoping to go next year. **4. F:** When I have free time, I drive to the beach and walk along the shore. I feel so happy and relaxed. **5. M:** I can't wait for the holidays. My whole family gets together and we eat, and talk, and exchange presents. **6. M:** How are we ever going to send our children to college? Tuition is so expensive. **7. M:** I'm really sorry that I bought that used car. It has so many problems. **8. F:** I hate city life, the noise, the crowds, the traffic. Why can't we live on a farm? **9. F:** Why is he in jail? **M:** He robbed a bank. **10. F:** Did you pick up my prescription? **F:** Oh, no. I'm sorry. **11. M:** Are you still looking for a house? **F:** No, we're not. We owe too much money on our credit cards. After we pay off our cards, we'll start looking again. **12. F:** I can't believe that the governor is thinking of raising the sales tax. We already pay a 6 percent tax.

Page 72
9. Listen to two people give their views on different issues in their town. What is the man's view? What is the woman's view? Use the vocabulary from the box to write your sentences.
The police department
M: We need to hire more police officers. This town is growing and we only have ten officers.
W: Let's not expand the department. There is very little crime in town. The only crime last year was one stolen car.
Youth center
M: There's nothing for our young people to do at night. This town should build a youth center.
W: We don't need a youth center. The young people should be able to use the high school facilities at night.
Library
M: The library in this town is in terrible condition. Let's tear it down and build a new one.
W: The library in this town is in terrible condition. Let's renovate it and add an addition.
Salary for the mayor
M: The mayor works hard. But the job is an honorary job and it's part time. The mayor shouldn't receive a salary.
W: The mayor works hard. How are we going to attract a good mayor for free? We need to pay the mayor a part-time salary.

Unit 13: Business and Industry
Page 78
Listen and write the questions. Then, read each question and circle the correct answer.
1. What language is spoken in Brazil? **2.** Which country is known for the Volga River? **3.** Where is the Grand Canyon located? **4.** Where is the richest gold mine located? **5.** Where is the bullet train ridden? **6.** Which country is bordered by Spain? **7.** Which currency is used in China? **8.** Which state is the most populated? **9.** How often are the Summer Olympics held? **10.** Where are the most films produced? **11.** How often is a U.S. president elected? **12.** Which city is the most populated? **13.** Why is July Fourth celebrated in the United States? **14.** Where is the World Cup held?

Unit 14: Technology Today
Page 84
6. Write each question you hear next to the correct answer.
1. Which bank was robbed? **2.** What time was the bank robbed? **3.** Was anyone injured? **4.** How much money was stolen? **5.** How was the thief dressed? **6.** When was the thief arrested? **7.** Where was he found?

Page 84
7. Listen to this report of a snowstorm in Cleveland, Ohio. How was the city affected?
Cleveland is digging out of one of their heaviest snowstorms in the past twenty years. Residents are shoveling out of over two feet of snow. At 7:00 this morning, the governor declared a state of emergency. All schools and colleges were closed. Banks and businesses were shut down. All flights in and out of the airport were cancelled and hundreds of people were stranded at the airport. They spent the night sleeping on cots, chairs, and on the floor. Mail delivery was suspended as postal workers were unable to reach their jobs. Only emergency vehicles were allowed on the streets.

Page 84
8. Listen to this report of a forest fire. Then, answer the questions.
Forest fires in the West continued to spread today and have now destroyed over 1000 acres. The fire reached the town of Stanton this afternoon. At 10:00 this morning, all one hundred residents of this small town were told to evacuate. They were given two hours to pack their cars and drive to safer areas. Fire fighters were able to save more than 30 homes, but they watched as more than 15 other homes were destroyed by the fire. Three fire fighters were injured when they were hit by a falling tree. There is one note of hope. Heavy rain is predicted for tomorrow and Thursday.

Unit 15: Country Music
Page 90
7. Listen and fill in the adjective clauses.
1. Bono is the lead singer for U-2, which is one of the most popular bands of all time. **2.** Bono was born in Ireland, where he was also raised. **3.** Bono and a group of other high-school students formed a band, which is now known as U-2. **4.** Bono tries to write songs whose lyrics are passionate. **5.** Bono likes to talk about music with his fans, whom he tries to inspire.

Page 90
8. Listen and take notes in the space below about Bono and U-2.
Paul Hewson, or "Bono," is known for his band, U-2, one of the most popular bands of all time, but he is also known for his political activities. Bono, was born in 1960. He was raised in Dublin, Ireland. When he was fifteen years old, his mother died suddenly. During the time after his mother's death, Bono became interested in music and began playing the guitar. It was during high school that one of his friends nicknamed him "Bono." In school, Bono was good at history and art, and he enjoyed performing and singing on stage with the school theater group.

In 1976, Bono and a group of other students formed a band, which is now known as U-2. Bono became the lead singer even though he wasn't the best singer of the group. It was his personality, his ability at songwriting, and his ability to perform on stage that gave him the job as lead singer and songwriter for the band.

Over the years, Bono's singing has matured and improved. His music is influenced by many kinds of music, from the opera that his father played when he was growing up to rap.

U-2's concerts are known for the fantastic performances. Bono tries to write songs whose lyrics are passionate and will inspire his fans. He expresses his ideas and opinions, and in each live performance, he wants to connect with his fans. He may even jump off of the stage and bring a fan up on the stage. And, it is not unusual to see Bono talking about music with fans on a city street.

Bono is a strong political activist. He has discussed world issues with Nelson Mandela in South Africa, with former president Clinton in the U.S., and with other world leaders. He is especially involved in causes for the poor and AIDS funding for Africa and donates money to a number of other social causes.